CORNWALL COUNTY COUNCIL
LIBRARIES AND ARTS DEPARTMENT

Cornish Heraldry and Symbolism

The Frontispiece

Arms of Godolphin. These may be blasoned or described in heraldic language as 'Gules, a double-headed eagle displayed between three fleurs-de-lys argent. Crest: a dolphin embowed proper'.

This is the most usual form in which a coat of arms is shown, comprising the shield, the helmet bearing the crest, the wreath or torse at the junction of the helmet and the crest, and the mantling or helmet drapery. Though there are many exceptions, it is usual for the torse and mantling to be depicted in the two main tinctures of the arms.

The dolphin crest is clearly intended as a pun on the family name, though the actual origin of this is quite different.

This book is number

....74...

of a limited edition

of 1000 copies

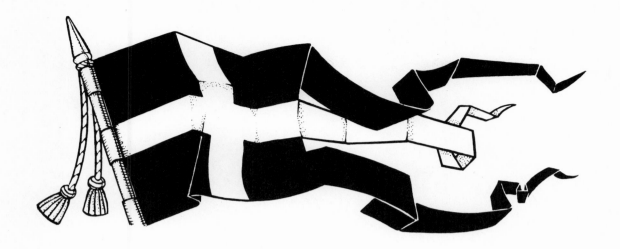

cornish heraldry
and symbolism

D.Endean
Ivall

To my dear wife Irene
for her practical and moral support

First published 1988

© *D. E. Ivall 1988*

ISBN 1-850220-433

Published by **Dyllansow Truran**
Cornish Publications
Trewolsta, Trewirgie, Redruth, Cornwall

Production Consultant: Anthony Wheaton
Tedburn St. Mary, Devon 0647-61329

Typeset by Exe Valley Dataset, Exeter, Devon

Printed by **Bookcraft Ltd**, *Midsomer Norton, Somerset*

Introduction

The aim of this work is to cover, or at least touch upon, the various aspects of symbolic and heraldic art associated with Cornwall, from the Roman-Celtic period to modern times. Clearly it would be impossible to describe or illustrate all the thousands of known devices in this wide field, but a representative selection is given in each category, and sources are indicated in which further examples may be found.

Collections of Cornish heraldry proper have been made since at least the 16th century, and members of the Cornish Guild of Heralds are at present working towards as complete as possible a record of the coats of arms and other devices used by individuals, families and bodies associated with Cornwall. Military devices of the many Cornish regular and volunteer units have been dealt with comprehensively by Charles Thomas and the present writer in 'Military Insignia of Cornwall'. There remain very many badges and emblems of Cornish cultural, educational, sporting and other bodies as yet insufficiently recorded.

The illustrations are in all cases either original drawings or re-drawings of items previously illustrated in manuscripts or published source material. The lay-out of the work is generally by category rather than chronological sequence, though there is inevitably some overlapping of the categories.

DENNIS ENDEAN IVALL   Perranwell, 1987

Abbreviations

R.I.C.	Royal Institution of Cornwall, River Street, Truro.
C.R.O.	Cornwall Record Office, County Hall, Truro.
M.I.C.	'Military Insignia of Cornwall', Ivall/Thomas, 1974/6.
Lysons	'Magna Britannia', Vol. VI, D. and S. Lysons, 1810.
Baring Gould	'An Armory of the Western Counties', 1898, from 16th century manuscripts.
Doble	'Cornish Saints Series', Canon G. H. Doble.
Blight	'Churches of West Cornwall', J. T. Blight, 1885.
Bain	'Celtic Art: The Methods of Construction', George Bain, Reprint, 1951.
Mead	'Cornwall's Royal Engineers', Lt. Col. C. J. H. Mead, 1947.
J.S.A.H.R.	Journal of the Society for Army Historical Research.
D.C.L.I.Mus.	Duke of Cornwall's Light Infantry Museum, Bodmin.

Acknowledgements

Among those who have given me valuable advice and assistance I wish especially to mention the staff of the Royal Institution of Cornwall, the staff of Cornwall Record Office, Malcolm Stephens of Tywardreath, and Jan Gendall of Menheniot.

Thanks are also due to the many officers and members of civic bodies and associations who have supplied examples, illustrations and information.

Contents

Origins and Rationale

Since long before the invention of written language men have sought to identify themselves by means of individual and group symbols, expressing the basic dual wishes to be different from others and at the same time to belong to a recognisable group. This idea has found expression in the form of uniforms, vestments, and other formal garb, and more particularly in the use of distinctive devices, either worn on the person or erected or carried as totems, flags, etc. Similarly, the use of symbols has been a prominent feature of religious and political movements.

Some modern thought is against any idea of separating nations, classes and individuals, and certainly the former class connotations of heraldry proper have tended to discredit the subject in some eyes. Some nation states have for ideological reasons actually banned the use of personal heraldry, though the use of symbols of other types plays a large part in the life of these as in other communities. Similarly, some religious groups are to varying degrees opposed to the use of ritualism and symbolism, on the grounds that the symbols themselves may receive the veneration due to the ideas behind them.

Leaving aside these ethical questions, there is no doubt that the subject attracts interest very largely because of its artistic and historical aspects. Heraldry and symbolism are worthy of study as part of our social and artistic history, and even in the modern age they still have a part to play as a decorative and useful shorthand in national, social and commercial contexts. It is probably the very largely impersonal, material and technological aspects of modern life that have led so many to delve into such subjects as local and family history, hand-craft, folk-culture, and, along with these, symbolism.

Celtic Symbolism

Religious, tribal and individual symbols were used by the Celtic peoples, as by virtually all communities whether primitive or developed. The use of symbols and cult objects has been dealt with extensively by Anne Ross in 'Pagan Celtic Britain'. Arguing the existence of a largely shared body of belief and practice among all the Celtic peoples of Europe, she quotes many examples of cult objects and symbols, largely derived from natural forms. Clearly many of these occur also in other non-Celtic contexts. In some categories she quotes no actual British examples, but assumes that such would have existed. This being so it is not surprising that surviving Cornish examples are lacking in some cases, but it is fair to assume that in general the inhabitants of what is now Cornwall would have shared the customs and attitudes prevailing in the rest of Celtic Britain.

Thus, some illustrations in this section are included simply as representative of a general Celtic symbolism. Those artists and craftsmen who in modern times wish their work to have a Celtic flavour often include such motifs, just as they make use of the decorative and calligraphic styles of former Celtic cultures.

Cult Creatures include the Bull, Boar, Wolf, Stag, Fighting-Dog, Horse, Goose, Eagle, Fish and Serpent, each with its sometimes complicated symbolism, some being particularly associated with individual pagan deities.

Plant Symbolism is held to have been a significant part of Celtic thought. The Druidic practice of meeting in groves rather than in constructed temples seems well documented, but modern scholars have cast doubt on long-accepted ideas concerning practices involving the mistletoe. To what extent does this in fact grow on oak trees, and would it really be practicable to cut mistletoe with a sickle of gold?

fig. 1   The illustration is an original composition showing some of the most typical Celtic symbols.

The Oak, the Mistletoe and the Yew traditionally associated with Druidic worship and Celtic legend.

Cernunnos. A Celtic deity bearing horns. (Antefix tile, Dorchester, 1st–2nd cty. A.D.).

The Bull. Symbol of strength and virility. (Pictish stone carving, Burghead, Inverness).

The Boar. Described by Anne Ross as 'the cult animal par excellence of the Celts'. Appears as a crest on Celtic helmets. Esteemed both as a symbol of fighting spirit and as a vital source of food. (Pictish stone carving, Dores, Inverness).

The Stag. (Incised on slate. Tintagel—approximate dating 500–800 A.D.).

The Tree of Life. (Book of Kells, 8th–9th cty A.D.).

1.

The Human Head played a major part as a cult symbol of the Celts, both as a battle-trophy in the form of the actual head of an enemy, and as representing human intelligence and supernatural powers.

Typical Decorative Motifs of Celtic Art and Craft were the Tryskel, the Spiral, Continuous Interlacing and Knotwork Panels. It is often difficult to separate pure decoration from symbolism, but from what we know of earlier cultures it is probably safe to assume that if a decorative element was capable of a symbolic interpretation its users were conscious of such.

The Tryskel and Spiral and similar circular motifs have been said to represent the sun, and the continuous interlaced line to represent the continuity of life.

These motifs, particularly interlacing and knotwork, often appear in later Scandinavian and Saxon work, though it is probable that much of the craft work associated with these cultures was either executed by Celtic craftsmen or directly inspired by them.

fig. 2   **Three-line Interlacing.** (Cross at Lanherne).

fig. 3   **Two-line Interlacing.** (Cross at Cardinham).

fig. 4   **Knotwork Motifs.** (Cross at Sancreed).

fig. 5   **Key Pattern.** (Cross at Sancreed).

fig. 6   **Three-line Interlacing.** (Cross at Phillack).

fig. 7   **Plait-work.** (Cross at Cardinham).

fig. 8   **Spiral Series.** (Cross at Cardinham).

fig. 9   **Tryskel.** Pictish. (Bain).

fig. 10   **Zoomorphic Spiral.** Cotton MS Vespasian A.1. (Bain).

The Serpent or Dragon was seen as a symbol of sovereignty and in various forms has continued in this and other contexts up to the present time. In early examples it is represented as being snake-like, without legs but often winged. Later forms are the Wyvern, a two-legged dragon, and the four- legged dragon, well known as the emblem of Wales.

fig. 12   In his imaginative 'History of the Kings of Britain', Geoffrey of Monmouth describes Arthur as bearing a gold dragon on his helmet, and mediaeval illustrations to the Arthur legends show a snake-like dragon as his standard.

In his 'Prophecies of Merlin', Geoffrey refers to two dragons in combat, one, coloured red, representing the British, and the other, coloured white, representing the invading Anglo-Saxons.

4

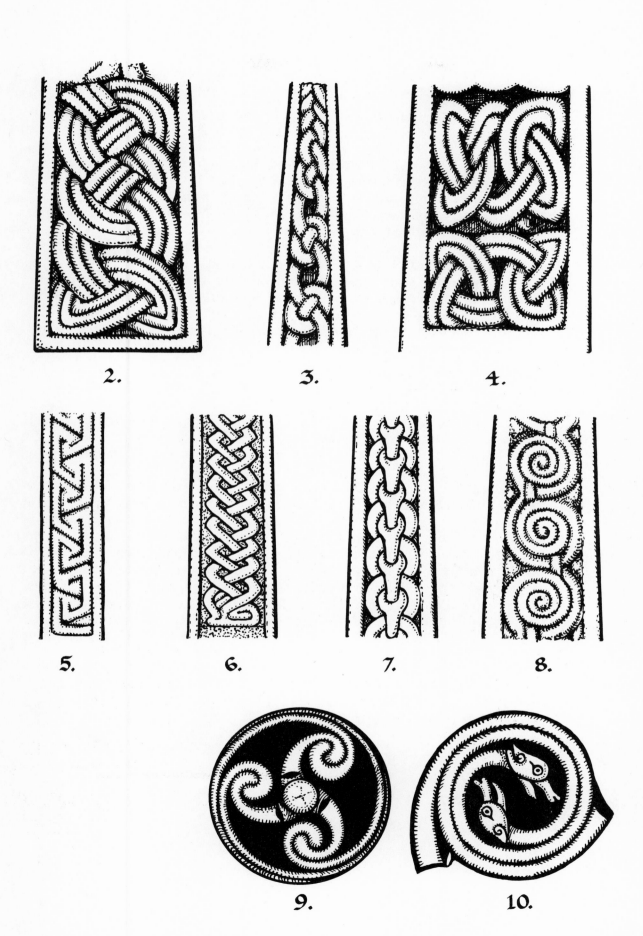

2. 3. 4.

5. 6. 7. 8.

9. 10.

Attributed or Legendary Coats of Arms

Mediaeval Heralds could not imagine a period when prominent men did not display armorial bearings, and consequently they invented such for many historical figures living long before the advent of true heraldry in the 12th century. Similarly, traditional figures whose very existence may in some cases be doubted were supplied with 'posthumous' coats of arms. Thus we see, in mediaeval and later rolls of arms, devices for the Nine Worthies of Christendom, and Alfred the Great and other Anglo-Saxon monarchs.

In the same way many arms were devised for saints and biblical figures, the designs in many cases alluding more or less directly to legends associated with them or to events in the scriptures. Even in modern times it is occasionally necessary to create such devices for inclusion in church decoration, etc., where none is already known for the saint in question.

Arthur. Whether he be regarded as war leader, king or god, Arthur has occupied a prominent place in the traditions of Britain. Although seen by many as a symbol of Celtic resistance to Anglo-Saxon domination, he was nevertheless adopted by the English as typifying the ancient spirit of Britain as a whole. Although he was credited with deeds performed throughout Britain, it is in the West of Britain and particularly in Cornwall that legend and popular imagination have set his homeland.

fig. 11   King Uther Pendragon, the legendary father of Arthur, had attributed to him various devices which included one or more dragons allusive to his name or title. Arthur himself was credited with several devices. Among these was a

fig. 12   green shield bearing a white cross, and in the first quarter the figure of Our Lady bearing the Christ Child in gold. Separate legendary accounts describe Arthur as bearing in battle the Cross of Christ and the image of the Virgin, which no doubt suggested the design of these arms to the mediaeval heralds. Similar arms are used by the town of Glastonbury, long associated with the Arthur legend. Among other devices attributed to Arthur is that of three gold

fig. 13   crowns on a red shield, no doubt in allusion to the various kingdoms he is claimed to have conquered.

'Nyns Yu Marow Myghtern Arthur' (Cornish—King Arthur is Not Dead). This refers to the persistent belief in his return, and is one of the mottoes of the Federation of Old Cornwall Societies whose chief aim is the preservation of all aspects of Cornish/Celtic tradition and culture.

11

13

NYNS YU MAROW MYGHTERN ARTHUR

12

Cornish/Celtic Saints

Although many of these are little more than names to us, others have had picturesque legends attached to them. In these legends there may well be elements of truth, but at this distance in time it is virtually impossible to distinguish fact from fiction. In some cases these legends have given rise to symbols which have come to be recognised as the devices of particular saints.

St Perran/Piran. He has been confused with the Irish Ciaran of Saighir, and has had many of this latter saint's legends attached to him. Thus we often see Perran represented with the millstone on which he is supposed to have floated from Ireland. (Doble).

fig. 14   However, it is as the Patron of Cornish tinners, and of Cornwall itself, that he is most widely known. Certainly his traditional device, a black banner bearing a white cross (sable, a cross argent) could not be bettered as a striking emblem of the Cornish people. It has been said to symbolise the triumph of good over evil, while others have seen in it a representation of bright refined tin contrasted with dark tin ore. The latter meaning was referred to by Davis Gilbert, the 19th century Cornish historian, when he described the flag as 'formerly the banner of St Perran, and the standard of Cornwall'.

This flag is not of course that of the Duchy of Cornwall, an estate and title which does not co-extend with Cornwall itself and which has its own well-known device of fifteen besants on a black ground. Cornwall County Council, too, has its own distinguishing device, being the arms of the Duchy within a border bearing blue and white waves. The County Council makes the distinction by flying both its own banner and that of St Piran.

The St Piran banner may be taken to represent the land of Cornwall and all those who consider themselves to be Cornish by domicile or by descent.

St Petrock. Although he has been described as the principal saint of Cornwall his influence has spread far and wide, particularly into what is now the English county of Devon where there are many churches dedicated to him. In fact, some have claimed, at least in modern times, that Petrock is the patron saint of Devon, so we may fairly leave him to fill this post, while recognising his firm links with Cornwall and Brittany also.

Associated with a number of saints of the Celtic Church, and others further afield, are legends concerning the protection of a deer from a hunter. Thus, Petrock is said to have saved a stag from the tyrant Constantine, whom he later converted. (Doble.) The whole story is illustrated on a carved stone shield in the late 15th century manor house of Rialton, the summer residence of the priors of Bodmin. Subscribed 'Petroc', this shows a stag, a hunting dog,

fig. 15   and the horn, crown and sword of Constantine. An actual horn, allegedly that of Constantine, was preserved as a relic in mediaeval times. This device is used by St Petroc's Church of England Infants' School at Bodmin.

Another device of Petrock appears on a shield among the carved

fig. 16   decoration surrounding the East window of the parish church of Padstow. This design includes a sword and two crowned objects of uncertain identity. The latter have been described as bows and arrows, but it seems more likely that each represents a Gothic letter P for Petroc.

S.PERRAN

14

15

S.PETROC

16

Heraldry Proper

Works on the history and the technicalities of heraldry may be found in any public library, and it is not proposed to deal with these at length here.

Although personal and communal symbols were used in war and peace from time immemorial, heraldry as a more or less organised system of hereditary shield devices came into general use only around the middle of the 12th century, and specifically in Europe.

Originally adopted by the great landowners and military leaders, which two categories covered to a large extent the same individuals, the idea spread to include all who could claim to be of the upper or 'gentle' class. Later, this class came to include wealthy merchants and some professions, and the borderline between the 'gentle' and 'simple' classes was always fluctuating. Coats of arms came to be used on seals, to authenticate documents, as marks of ownership on personal possessions, and as decoration on buildings, memorials, etc. These peaceful uses led to the adoption of heraldic and quasi-heraldic emblems by religious bodies, trade guilds, civic authorities and others in non-military contexts. In continental Europe there was widespread use of heraldry by all classes, including the lesser merchants, craftsmen and farmers. Such arms come under the general classification of 'burgher' arms, as distinct from those used by families who were technically 'noble' or 'gentle', or at least claimed to be such.

The heralds, officers knowledgeable in the fields of genealogy, coats of arms and ceremonial, particularly in relation to tournaments, were maintained by the Crown and the greater nobles, often being named after some title or possession of their lord. Thus, a certain John Hilton, harper, was appointed 'Cornwall Herald' by Richard II. He is mentioned in 1398–9 and again at the coronation of Henry V in 1413. However he apparently had no specific duties associated with Cornwall, simply deriving his title from the Duchy held by the Heir Apparent. One Cornish family at least had its own heraldic officer, Sir Richard Nanfan, Lord Deputy of Calais in 1503, retained a pursuivant or junior herald named Serreshal.

For the most part Cornish heraldry conformed to the rules and customs prevailing in England, which in turn followed in a general way the practices of continental Europe. The following quotations do however suggest that the use of arms was possibly more prevalent here among less prominent families, and that the general control of heraldry was somewhat looser, Cornwall being remote from the seat of government.

Richard Carew, in his 'Survey of Cornwall' of 1602, says 'One John Luff, author of a small accidens of armory —— of no great value except for some arms of Cornish gentlemen, *hardly to be met with elsewhere*, taken out of church windows, etc. I have it now by me in MS.' Elsewhere Carew writes, 'The Cornish appear to change and diversify their arms at pleasure'! And again, 'The most Cornish gentlemen can better vaunt of their pedigree than their livelihood for that they derive from great antiquity, and I make question whether any shire in England of but equal quantitie can muster a like number of faire Coate-Armours'.

Jewers, in his 'Heraldic Church Notes from Cornwall', c. 1860–80, refers to a number of small landowners using arms which were never registered with the College of Arms in London. Gayre, in 'Gayre's Booke', 1948, refers to the great number of ancient Cornish coats of arms coloured black and white, 'considered Cornish colours', and quotes Lake's 'Parochial History of Cornwall' to the same effect. Michael Trinnick, in the guide to Trerice, near Newquay, says, '16th century Cornwall, remote from the court and the capital, had few great seats. Further, the Duchy being annexed to the crown, the Chief Lord of the County was permanently absent. On the other hand, there existed a considerable number of small but prosperous gentry who farmed their own land, put their younger sons to trade, and formed an active hard-working upper class. Nearly every large farm or barton housed its "Gentleman of Coat Armour".'

The essential feature of a coat of arms is that it should be distinctive, that is, different from others in use. Any symbolic significance in the devices chosen is incidental, though of course of considerable interest. One of the most frustrating aspects of heraldry is the inability to know what prompted the choice of a particular design, if we assume that this was other than mere whim.

Many fanciful tales are told to account for the origin of some arms, but these are very often invented long after the adoption of the design, being based on romantic speculation rather than sound evidence. In some cases the intention is clear, that is, to illustrate the family name by some appropriate device, or to 'pun' on the name regardless of its true meaning. Contrary to popular belief, there are comparatively few authenticated instances of arms, or additions to them, being granted for specific services or exploits.

Legal Aspects

Much debate has taken place over the legality or propriety of assuming arms for oneself. It is generally accepted that this was normal practice in the early days of heraldry, the only limitation being the practical one of ensuring that the design adopted was distinctive, and moreover easily recognisable from a distance. As the Crown, through its heraldic officers, began to claim control, succeeding to a greater or lesser extent at different periods, the view came to be held that only such arms as were recorded and recognised by these officers could be considered valid, a view naturally fostered by the heralds themselves.

Certainly in Tudor and Stuart times the Heralds of the English College of Arms received royal commissions to 'visit' all parts of the kingdom to register and confirm arms, and to 'put down' those which they considered to be borne without sufficient authority. Their criteria varied, and many arms which had simply been assumed in the past were allowed if the claimant was accepted as being of appropriate social status.

These powers have long been disused, and in spite of an attempted revival of the Court of Chivalry (one case in 1954) the English College of Arms now makes no attempt at control. Thousands of unregistered arms, devices, badges, flags, etc., are used by individuals and associations in Cornwall alone. This is in contrast to Scotland where there is proper legislation and full legal power for Lyon King of Arms to control heraldic matters.

Throughout the whole period of attempted control and up to modern times the assumption of arms has continued in Britain (apart from Scotland) as it has in most European countries, and more recently worldwide. The argument between official control and free assumption has sometimes been fierce, with equally learned heraldists supporting one or other view, but from a practical standpoint there is nothing to prevent anyone assuming arms.

In these days the dangers resulting from duplication of coats of arms used on the battle-field, or on seals appended to legal documents, hardly apply. However, good manners and respect for heraldic traditions should prevent anyone from adopting arms identical with any previously granted or in use, or from claiming arms by inheritance without sufficient genealogical evidence.

In the 18th and 19th centuries a great number of families attaining or claiming some social standing used coats of arms or crests to decorate their stationery, signet rings, carriages, silver, etc., and it is safe to say that the great majority of these devices were never officially registered. Sometimes such a family would obtain an official grant, but the Heralds' Visitations having ceased and the Court of Chivalry being practically if not technically defunct, many more simply assumed the devices of other families with the same or similar name, or adopted new ones. At that period the use of a crest alone was very common, though a crest cannot now properly exist unless there is also a coat of arms which relates to it. It is probably this widespread usage which led to the misuse of the word 'crest' as applied to any type of badge or device, and even to a complete coat of arms.

An act of 1798 required anyone displaying any such device on a carriage, or in any other public fashion, to obtain a licence on payment of a fee of one or two guineas. In a sense this condoned the use of unregistered devices, as the act required one to obtain a licence whether they were officially granted or not. The act was repealed in 1945, presumably because the cost of administering it was not justified by the amount raised.

Modern supporters of the Stannary laws of Cornwall would no doubt claim that still, as in the past, tinners and 'adventurers' or investors in the tin industry are exempt from action in the courts other than the Stannary courts in any matter not concerning 'life, limb or land'. It is very unlikely that anyone ever claimed this privilege as against the Court of Chivalry in a matter of bearing a coat of arms, though there is little doubt that such a claim would have been found valid.

Even at the period of most effective Crown control many individuals and bodies adopted devices of a more or less heraldic character without such use being challenged. Among these were merchants' marks, somewhat akin to the modern trademark, and rebuses or pictorial devices, usually punning on the name. It is certain that a registered trademark enjoys a legal protection denied to personal heraldry.

We have nowadays to consider that a great many families of Cornish descent are domiciled world-wide in areas which have their own heraldic establishments or have none. Thus such a family wishing to obtain an official grant may choose to approach the heraldic authorities of, say, Spain or South Africa, or elsewhere according to their domicile, rather than apply to the English College of Arms.

Sources for Cornish Heraldry

The sources for research into Cornish heraldry are many and varied. There are several printed works which give details of British arms in general, from which Cornish arms may be extracted.

A useful list of sources is given in 'A Cornish Armory' (Pascoe/Ivall, 1979), and Cornwall Record Office has published a handlist of most of the heraldic material deposited there.

Burke's 'General Armory', the latest and best edition published in 1884, gives some tens of thousands of arms with the relevant family name, and in some cases the location and/or biographical and historial details, etc. Sources are rarely quoted but are said to include the Heralds' Visitations, ancient rolls of arms, miscellaneous MSS, and church monuments. This work is initially helpful when searching for a family's arms but contains many errors due to mis-readings. It can also be very frustrating when arms are described for a particular name without additional information. Burke included all arms known to him whether or not they were officially granted or recorded. Needless to say, any arms mentioned as being associated with a particular name are not the property of all bearers of that name. Other Burke publications, such as The Peerage and Landed Gentry, give the arms of prominent families together with relevant pedigrees.

'Fairbairn's Crests', of the late 19th century gives the name, crest and motto, if any, and occasionally identifies the family by location, as well as providing illustrations.

The great majority of arms and other devices known to have been used by individuals and bodies associated with Cornwall have been indexed by the Cornish Guild of Heralds, and this work continues in respect of newly adopted devices or those previously in use which come to light from time to time.

Malcolm Stephens has recently produced a useful 'Ordinary' for most of the better known Cornish arms, classifying them according to the elements in their design. This enables one to identify un-named arms found out of context.

Sources of many of the individual devices illustrated in this present work are referred to in the text. Some of these sources cannot be termed 'authorities' for the bearing of particular devices, but are nevertheless evidence that they were or are actually in use.

Enquiries as to the existence of arms for a particular family, if local sources fail, may be made to The College of Arms in London, or where appropriate, to the Lyon Office in Edinburgh or the Genealogical Office in Dublin. These bodies will of course charge fees for searching their records, the amount depending on the work involved and not on the successful result of the search. Generally speaking, they deal only with arms which have been officially recognised by them.

Mediaeval Military Leaders & Landowners

Some enthusiasts have claimed that the only 'true' heraldry is that which was used on the mediaeval battle-field. This is rather a limited view of the subject, but that period certainly provides us with examples of heraldry at its best. Most of the early arms were of very simple and distinctive design, fitting their purpose, and far removed from some of the extravagancies of later years. Clearly it was easier to design simple but distinctive arms at a time when a comparatively limited number of individuals required them.

fig. 17   **Carminow, of St Mawgan in Meneage.** The stone effigy in the parish church is typical of many which show us the dress and equipment of a knight of the period, c. 1300. The effigy is badly worn and defaced, and the illustration is partly a reconstruction based on similar monuments elsewhere. However, the most distinctive feature is quite clear, that is the small

fig. 18   triangular shield with a plain 'bend', or diagonal band.

fig. 19   Illustrated along with the original arms are 'differenced' versions adopted

fig. 20   by branches of the family.

    The difficulties arising when two or more individuals claimed the same arms are illustrated by a classic controversy which occurred in the 14th century. A Cornish knight, a member of this same Carminow family, was challenged to prove his right to bear the very simple arms, 'azure, a bend or', that is, a blue shield bearing a diagonal gold band. These same arms were claimed by two unrelated English knights, one of whom maintained that his family had used the device from the time of the Norman Conquest. Carminow for his part testified that the arms had been granted to his family in the time of King Arthur! At neither period was there such a thing as an inheritable coat of arms, but the council of knights hearing the case accepted both testimonies. It was, and still is, the rule that no two individuals of the same nation should bear identical arms, and one of the English knights was obliged to adopt a different device. The other was allowed to retain the old arms, and Carminow too was allowed to continue their use. As was stated in the records of the case, Cornwall was in effect a separate country, 'a large land formerly bearing the name of a kingdom'. (Misc. Rolls of Chanc. Nos 311 and 312.)

    Strictly speaking no two individuals, even if related, should bear absolutely identical arms, but the practice of 'differencing' between members of the same family is now largely discontinued, except in Scotland.

17

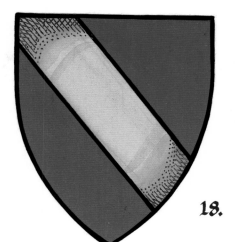

18.

19.

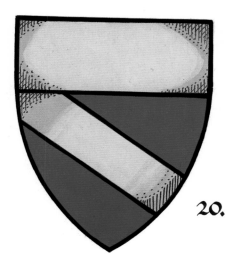

20.

Long before heraldry proper appeared seals were used by prominent individuals to authenticate documents, and for this purpose they needed to be of distinctive design. Thus, soon after heraldic devices began to be adopted by military leaders, they also appeared on the seals of the greater landowners. Such seals eventually came to be used by lesser notables, churchmen, religious foundations and craft associations.

fig. 21   **Robert de Cardinan.** (Temp. Richard II). This is typical of early seals bearing a single device, not on a shield, and preceding the true heraldic types.

fig. 22   **Sir John de Dynham.** (Temp. Richard II). A simple triangular shield with the arms, (gules) four fusils conjoined in fesse (argent), framed in Gothic tracery.

fig. 23   **Sir John Arundell.** (Temp. Henry VI). This shows a complete coat of arms, with helmet and crest in addition to the shield. These accoutrements are shown much as they would have appeared in actual use. The shield is quartered to combine the arms of Arundell with those of the allied family of Carminow. The six 'hirondelles' or swallows allude to the name, and the wolf alludes to an alliance with the Trembleth family. These latter again are punning arms, 'blyth' being Cornish for wolf. (See also fig. 146.) The helm is the tilting or tournament type of the 14th century, with a scalloped mantling or protective cloth. The wolf crest is set on a 'cap of maintenance' trimmed with ermine, a mark of high rank. The whole is accompanied by foliage and Gothic tracery.

These illustrations are re-drawn from engravings in Lysons 'Magna Britannia', 1810.

21

22

23

17

The Church

Symbolism and religion have always gone hand in hand, and the Christian Church has throughout its history made use of pictorial symbols to promote its message. Of particular value for the instruction of largely illiterate followers, symbolic art and craft work have also provided an outlet for both creative genius and the sacrifice of wealth in the cause of worship.

The cross was a decorative motif long before it came to be recognised as a Christian symbol, but thereafter was used universally as such in craft work of all kinds. In Cornwall, as elsewhere in Celtic Britain, it often appeared on a monolith or standing stone. Many of these are stated to be of pagan origin, later carved with a cross head. More were newly erected, bearing the cross in a number of forms ranging from the crudest shallow indication to the more elaborate wheel-cross, bearing interlaced and other decoration. Other examples include the crucifix itself. Occasionally the cross head is partly or completely pierced by four holes leaving either the usual upright cross form or a 'saltire' with the arms arranged diagonally.

An early Christian symbol allied to the cross was the Chi-Rho, consisting of these two Greek letters representing the name of Christ.

fig. 24   **Chi-Rho.** Complete letters. Early form. Phillack, 4th century.

fig. 25   **Chi-Rho.** Stylised later form. St Just. Early 6th century.

fig. 26   **Chi-Rho.** Stylised later form. St Endellion. c. 600 A.D.

fig. 27   **Cross-head.** 'Formy' or splayed type. Lanivet.

fig. 28   **Cross-head.** Four blind 'piercings'. Penlee Gardens, Penzance.

fig. 29   **Cross-head.** Three piercings, one part-piercing. Perranzabuloe. pre-960 A.D.

fig. 30   **Cross-head.** 'Hiberno-Saxon'. Crucifix. Sancreed.

fig. 31   **Cross-head.** Five bosses. 'Hiberno-Saxon'. Phillack. 10th cty.

fig. 32   **Cross-head.** A late example (13th cty?), part Celtic, part Gothic decoration. Quethiock.

The use of standing crosses was varied, some marking sacred sites, others boundaries or routes. Some were erected quite late in the Middle Ages.

(See 'Old Cornish Crosses', Arthur G. Langdon, 1896, and 'The Kingdom of Dumnonia', Susan Pearce, 1978.)

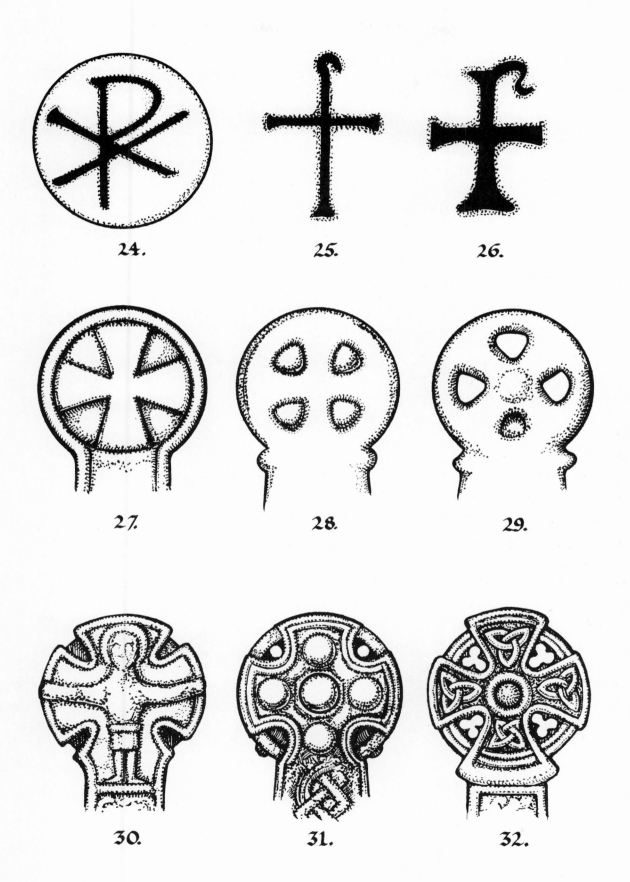

24.

25.

26.

27.

28.

29.

30.

31.

32.

fig. 33 **Tympanum, Perranarworthal.** Norman. The Agnus Dei, a lamb bearing a cross or cross-flag, was widely used in the Mediaeval Church as a symbol of Christ the sacrificial Lamb supporting the triumphant banner of the Resurrection. We also find this device used in Cornwall much later, as the mark of a number of tin-smelting houses.

fig. 34 **Font, Bodmin.** 12th cty. Baptism itself is a symbolic act, and the font is often decorated with appropriate symbols. Here the four winged heads can be seen as angelic protectors of the new-made Christian. The 'tree of life' is a traditional symbol in Celtic and other cultures. The beasts may represent fiends eager to seize on an unprotected soul.

fig. 35
fig. 36 **Bench-Ends, Mullion.** 16th cty. The carved decoration of bench-ends often included religious or secular emblems, and here we see the spear, sponge and nail-heads representing Christ's Passion, and the chalice and wafer of the Eucharist.

fig. 37 **Pulpit, Padstow.** c. 1530. The Five Wounds of Christ were a powerful symbol of the Passion, borne on banners by those taking part in the Western Rebellion of 1549. Such religious emblems were often depicted on shields, but only rarely, as in this example, with an accompanying helmet and mantling. The helmet also bears a crown of thorns instead of the usual wreath or 'torse' of entwined silk. This device may have been intended to represent the 'coat of arms' of Christ Himself, such an idea being quite acceptable to mediaeval and later thought.

33.

34.

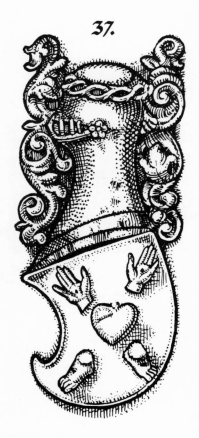

37.

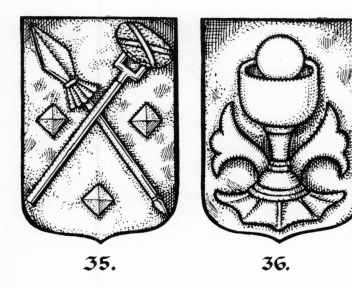

35.   36.

fig. 38   **Seal of St Lawrence's Hospital, Bodmin.** (Temp. Edward I?). The Saint is shown bearing the gridiron on which he is said to have suffered martyrdom. (Lysons)

fig. 39   **Arms of Bodmin Priory.** Carved on the tomb of Prior Thomas Vivian, 1533. These arms are sometimes erroneously stated to be those of Vivian.

fig. 40   **Seal of the Priory of St Stephen, Launceston.** (Temp. Henry VIII). A stylised representation of the Priory building. (Lysons)

fig. 41   **Seal of Archdeacon Phillpotts,** as Archdeacon of Cornwall, 1845–1889. St Michael, slaying the dragon, appears above a shield of the Phillpotts arms. At this period the Archdeaconry covered the whole of Cornwall, but on the establishment of the See of Truro in 1876 the two Archdeaconries of Bodmin (East Cornwall) and Cornwall (West Cornwall) were set up, their seals bearing respectively the figures of St Petrock and St Michael.

fig. 42   **Seal of Bishop Benson,** first Bishop of Truro, 1877. The arms of the Diocese of Truro impaling those of Benson.

    The current episcopal seal bears two separate shields with the arms of the diocese and those of the Bishop respectively, the mitre placed centrally above them. This arrangement is preferable where the two coats of arms are sufficiently complicated in themselves.

    Prelates do not now display helmets and crests with their arms, but a grant of arms to a bishop does include a crest, for use by his male descendants.

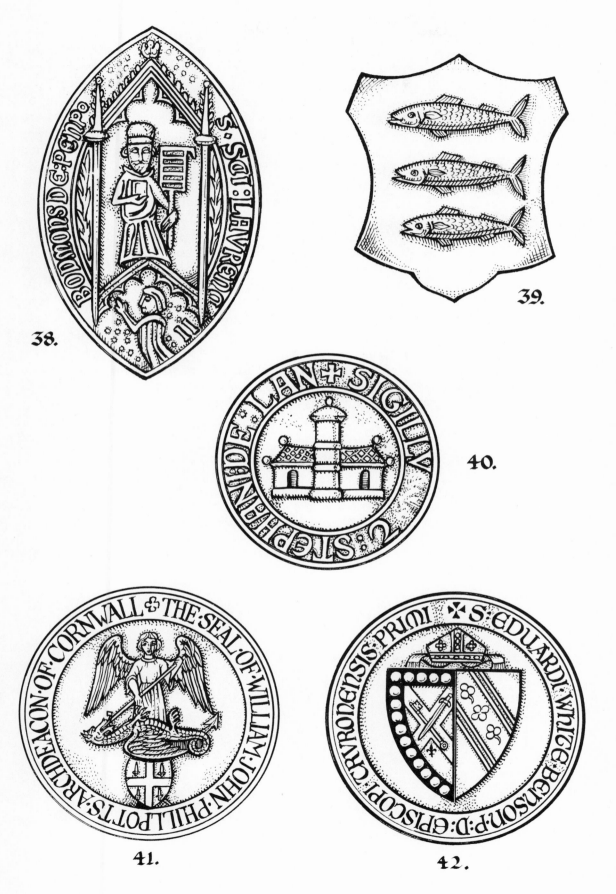

38.

39.

40.

41.

42.

23

fig. 43 **Truro Cathedral Banner.** The arms of the See of Truro include a 'St Patrick's' cross intended to represent the ancient Celtic Church. This cross, however, was only attributed to St Patrick when it was required for inclusion in the revised version of the Union Flag in 1801. A diagonal cross does, in fact, appear on the ancient standing stone sited at High Cross, before the Cathedral. The arms also include the sword of St Paul and the key of St Peter, derived from the device of the parent See of Exeter. Below these appears a fleur-de-lys representing the Blessed Virgin, to whom the Parish Church was dedicated. The shield bears the widely used black border with besants. Above the arms is the Bishop's mitre, and backing the whole is the Bishop's crozier, based on the form of a shepherd's crook and representing his pastoral care. In the flanks are the arms of the Priories of Bodmin and St Germans, the major religious houses of Cornwall.

The device of Holy Cross, Crediton, recalls the fact that Cornwall and Devon were separated from the ancient Diocese of Sherborne in 910 A.D. to form a new diocese with its seat at Crediton.

The four figures represent personages notable in the history of the Cornish Church. St Piran, one of the most widely revered saints of Celtic Cornwall, is here accompanied by the mill-stone on which he is said to have floated to Cornwall from Ireland. King Athelstan, having dominated the Cornish in 931 A.D., established a bishopric at St Germans. Henry Martyn, a descendant of a Cornish mining family, is noted for his missionary work in Persia and India. Edward Benson became the first Bishop of the new See of Truro in 1877, and later Archbishop of Canterbury.

S. Piran

King Athelstan

S. Mary Truro

Holy Cross Crediton

Hu. Martyn B.D.

Abp. Benson

43.

fig. 44 **St Agnes Mothers Union.** The banner bears the Mothers Union monogram, lilies representing the Madonna, and a lamb representing the innocence of the martyred St Agnes. The lamb (Latin—agnus) is also a play on the name.

fig. 45 **St Cornelly.** This device appears in a modern window in the tiny parish church of Cornelly, near Tregony. There may have been an earlier, Celtic, dedication, but the saint now honoured is the 3rd cty Pope and Martyr Cornelius. The patriarchal cross is combined with a horn, a pun on the name and a reference to the saint as the patron of horned beasts. ('Saints, Signs and Symbols', W. Ellwood Post, 1965.)

fig. 46 **Prebendal Foundation of St Endellion.** This ancient body obtained a grant of arms in 1950, illustrating the legend of St Endelienta. Included are her virgin's crown, her cow miraculously restored to life, the hill on which the church was built, and the heifers who drew her body on a cart. The actual grant is displayed in the parish church.

fig. 47 **Perranarworthal Parish Church.** The banner shows St Perran bearing his staff and bell, before the cross that stands near his oratory at Perranzabuloe. Prominent in the design is the device of a white cross on a black ground, and the whole is surrounded by Celtic interlacing. The saint's staff and bell were listed among relics surviving up to the Reformation.

44.

45.

46.

47.

In Memoriam

Featured in many of our parish churches are memorials to prominent local individuals. Some are of great artistic and architectural merit, and those that include effigies provide valuable evidence of the costume of the period, either military or civil. Many memorials include the coats of arms of the deceased together with those of allied families.

Following the age-old custom of burying a warrior's weapons and armour with him, it was the practice in mediaeval times, and to a lesser extent in succeeding centuries, to parade the dead man's helmet, shield, banner and other accoutrements in the funeral procession. Some of these items would later be hung in the church as permanent memorials. Often the items paraded would be specially made for the ceremonial, rather than those actually used in warfare. Unfortunately a number of these memorial helmets and other items have been stolen from our churches, as they have become desirable to collectors of militaria.

A custom which has persisted from Tudor times even into the present age was the carrying of a 'hatchment' or lozenge-shaped panel bearing the arms of the deceased. Often the arms of the marriage partner were included in the design, and the extent to which the background was blackened or left white indicated which, if either, survived.

The ceremonial of the funerals of persons of note was largely in the hands of the Heralds, and this practice continues in the case of State Funerals today.

fig. 48   **Memorial Brass. Geoffrey St Aubyn.** 1400. (Crowan). He appears in the full plate armour of the period, resting his feet on a lion.

fig. 49   **Memorial Brass. James Eryssey.** 1522. (Grade). He appears in the 'Gothic' armour of the Tudor period. The arms are one of several versions used by this family.

fig. 50   **Memorial Brass. Thomas Aumarle, Rector.** c. 1400. (Cardynham). He is shown in civilian/clerical costume. Again, the arms are one of several versions used.

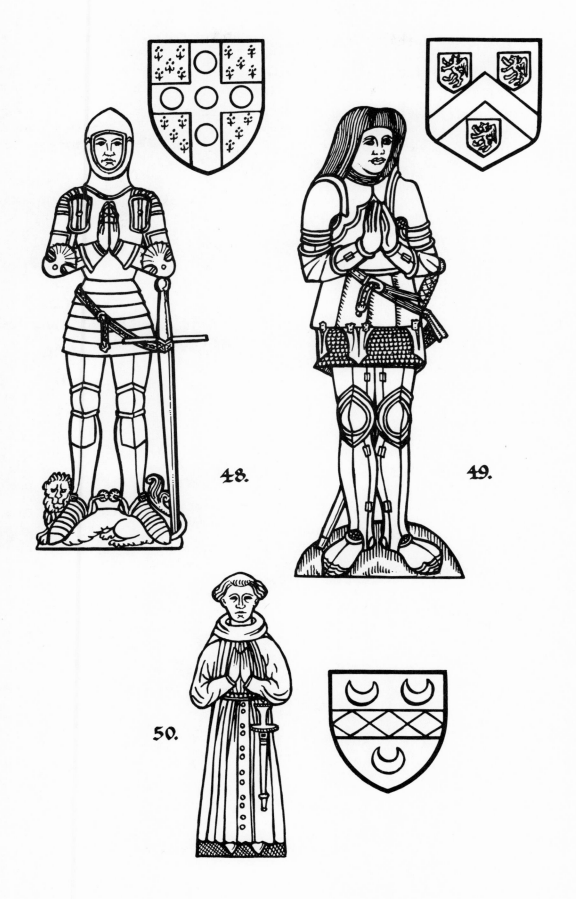

48.

49.

50.

fig. 51   **Memorial Brass. John Arundel, d. 1545.** (St Columb Major). This shows two multi-quartered shields, each displaying the Arundel arms with five other quarterings of allied families. Each shield also shows on the sinister side the arms of one of his two wives, Elizabeth Grey and Catherine Grenville.★ These latter are also combined with quarterings representing families allied to them.

fig. 52   **Memorial Brass. John Boscawen of Tregothnan.** 1564. (St Michael Penkevil). Typically of many memorials this shows the deceased at prayer, and in this case dressed in the armour of the period. The arms are those still borne by the Boscawens of Tregothnan.

fig. 53   **Memorial Brass. John Killigrew.** 1567. (St Budock). The arms of Killigrew, with helmet, crest and mantling. The shield bears the quarterings of Killigrew and seven allied families.

fig. 54   **Funerary Helmet.** Breage. Bearing the dolphin crest of Godolphin.

★*N.B.* 'Dexter' and 'sinister' relate to the right and left sides of a shield from the point of view of one carrying it, not of the onlooker.

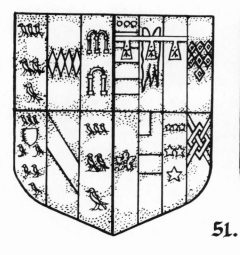
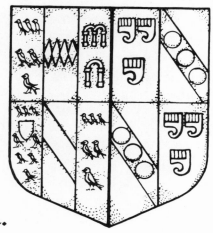

51.

52.

53.

54.

fig. 55   **Memorial to John Mayow of Polruan.** d. 1645. Carved in low relief on a stone slab. These arms have been used by many families of the name Mayow, Mayhew, May, etc. The crescent was often used as a mark of difference to show a second son, or a member of a line descended from such.

fig. 56   **Monument to Henry Spoure.** d. 1688. (Northill). The oval shield with accompanying scroll-work is typical of a 17th century style, far removed from the heraldry of the battlefield. The Spoure arms occupy the first of the many quarterings but are virtually lost in the general patchwork effect. The crest features one of heraldry's fabulous creatures, the 'heraldic antelope'.

fig. 57   **Hatchment.** 1770. (St Erney). The Blake arms 'impaling' those of Smith. The black background to the former indicates that he pre-deceased his wife.

fig. 58   **Hatchment.** 1871/2. (Fowey). The arms of William Rashleigh of Menabilly impaling those of his wife Catherine Stewart. The whole of the background being blacked-out signified that both husband and wife were deceased. It is possible that the hatchment was used firstly for him, with the background to the wife's arms left white, and that this was blacked-out for use at her funeral the following year.

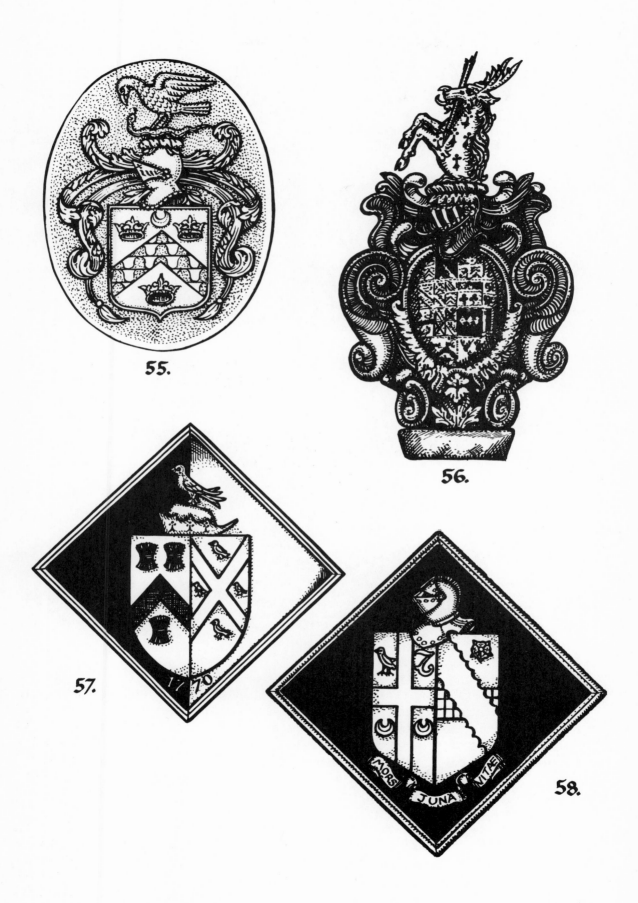

55.

56.

57.

58.

59

fig. 59 **Vyvyan of Trelowarren.** The arms and the crest both allegedly allude to the ancient legend of the submerging of the land of Lyonesse. An ancestor of the family is said to have narrowly escaped the flood on horseback, and in later years it was believed that a saddled horse was held in readiness for another such emergency. The base is sometimes shown as a green mound.

The arms bear the device of a baronet of England, a red sinister hand, derived from the red dexter hand of Ulster, the fees required of the original baronets having been used to finance the settlement of that province.

The open helmet is of the type officially reserved from the end of the 17th century to distinguish the arms of knights and baronets, and was further required to be shown full-face. This limitation often causes difficulties when the crest is represented in profile, and the rules as to the style of helmet and the direction in which it faces are nowadays often disregarded.

CALA RAG WHETHLOW

60

fig. 60 **Carminow.** Adapted from the memorial in Lanhydrock Church to George Carminow of Polmaugen, d. 1599.

The arms of Carminow are quartered with those of Lower. George's wife Jane was the heiress of George Lower, and thus these quartered arms could be borne by their descendants.

The supporters were not officially recorded, and some doubt exists as to their identity. That on the dexter is sometimes described as an eagle, but is actually a pelican in its heraldic form, wounding its own breast. That on the sinister has been variously described as a parrot, chough or dove!

Trevanion and Trevenen

fig. 61   **Trevanion.** The practice of the English College of Arms has been to limit the use of supporters, the figures flanking a shield, to certain degrees such as peers and Knights Grand Cross of Orders of Chivalry. The Trevanions however, like the Carminows, are one of a number of long- established families in Cornwall and elsewhere who used supporters over a considerable period.

The arms shown illustrate how families of the same or similar names have adopted, or have been granted, arms of very similar design. This ought to imply that there is a proved or probable blood relationship, but this cannot be taken for granted. The origins of the Trevanion and Trevenen families are generally held to be quite distinct, the former being said to derive from trev-Enyon (Enyon's homestead), and the latter from tre-venen (the woman's homestead). As with most place-names however actual proof of the origin is hard to come by.

Whatever the truth of the matter, the two families were using similar arms in the 16th century, as follows. (Baring Gould)

fig. 61   **Trevanion.** Argent, on a fesse azure, three escallops or, between two chevrons gules.

fig. 62   **Trevenen.** Argent, a fesse gules, between two chevrons azure.

The latter being the simpler design, one would normally assume that it was the earlier of the two to be adopted.

fig. 63   In the 18th century the Trevenen family obtained a new grant from the College of Arms. These arms differed somewhat from those anciently used, and resembled even more those of Trevanion. The wording of the grant actually states that a connection with Trevanion could be surmised because the names were similar and both families were of Cornwall. The grant makes no reference to the Trevenen arms already in use in the 16th century. The crest also closely resembles that of Trevanion, again being a quartered stag, but quartered in different colours.

en·dieu·est·mon·espoir

61　　　62　　　63

The Tudor Period

The Cornish and Welsh were prominent in bringing Henry Tudor to the throne, though his later policies and those of his successors often alienated the Cornish, and Wales soon lost its distinct identity as far as government and the law were concerned.

fig. 64   **Thomas Vivian,** Prior of Bodmin, was the most influential churchman in Cornwall of his time. Although all Vivians/Vyvyans of Cornwall were thought to have derived from the same stock, Prior Vivian adopted arms differing widely from those of the Trelowarren Vyvyans. The arms shown, carved on his tomb at Bodmin dated 1533, are typical of grants made in the Tudor period. Many ancient arms bore a motif represented three times, but as more families applied for grants it became increasingly difficult to devise arms sufficiently different from those in existence. Consequently we often find a pattern similar to that shown, i.e. three objects on a chevron between three others, with three more on a 'chief'.

fig. 65   **Thomas Flamank,** lawyer, of Bodmin, was one of the leaders of the Cornish Rebellion of 1497. The cross was a very frequently used device, in this case accompanied by four pierced 'mullets' or spur-rowels. The saracen's head was frequently used as a crest, and must often have been adopted with reference to some real or imagined crusading ancestor. Similarly, some Welsh families displayed severed Englishmen's heads in their arms!

fig. 66   **John Tregonwell,** also a lawyer, was Henry VIII's Proctor at the time of the latter's attempt to divorce his first wife Catherine. On the successful outcome of this affair, and for further services in disposal of confiscated Church property, he acquired the estate of Milton Abbey in Dorset. Choughs very naturally appeared in the arms of a good number of Cornish families. In this case the arms are distinguished by three black roundels. These could be intended to represent gun-stones or cannon-balls and could be a pun on the 'gon' element in the name. Presumably the actual origin of this is Cornish 'gun', meaning a down, but for the sake of the pun this origin would have been ignored, even if known.

fig. 67   **Francis Tregian,** of Wolvedon, near Probus, suffered as a recusant under Elizabeth, and is probably best known as the patron of Saint Cuthbert Mayne, martyred at Launceston. These arms appear in various different forms with the field of the shield shown as ermine, argent, or gold, and the birds described in different sources as choughs, jays, eagles or martlets.

64.

65.

66.

67.

King and Parliament

In the 17th century political and military conflict between Parliament and Crown the Cornish in the main supported the Royalist cause, and the Cornish army won many victories on the King's behalf. Nevertheless some prominent families and much of the population of East Cornwall were active on behalf of Parliament.

fig. 68   **Sir John Eliot,** famous as the champion of constitutional rights, was of the family of the Earls of St Germans. For his opposition to Charles I he was imprisoned in the Tower, where he died in 1632. The elephant crest of this family was no doubt adopted as a pun on the family name. The Scandinavian family Von Ely used virtually the same arms and crest, and a descent from the Cornish Eliots in the 17th century seems likely, though not proven, following recent research by the Norwegian genealogist Kolbørn Ekkje.

fig. 69   **Sir Bevil Grenville,** of the famous family seated at Stowe, was one of Charles's most successful generals. He was killed at the battle of Lansdowne Hill. The devices on these arms are variously described as 'clarions' or 'rests', being said to derive either from a type of military wind instrument or from a lance-rest such as was fixed to a horseman's breastplate.

fig. 70   **John Arundell of Trerice.** Many of this family made their marks in Cornish history, but here we commemorate the heroic defender of Pendennis, one of the last Royalist fortresses to fall. Various crests were used by different branches of this family, but the arms in each case included the punning 'hirondelles' or swallows.

fig. 71   **Lord (John) Robartes,** a member of a wealthy banking and tin trading family, was one of Parliament's most active supporters in Cornwall. The rampant lion is one of the most commonly used devices, both on a shield and as a crest, and usually needs to be differentiated by having some object in its paws, charged on the body or around the neck, etc.

68.

69.

70.

71.

The Order of the Garter

This, the senior English order of chivalry, has included relatively few Cornishmen as the honour has usually been reserved for prominent statesmen and members of the aristocracy, often of ducal rank. Cornwall, being considered practically a perquisite of the heir to the English throne, had few families of such prominence.

fig. 72   **Sidney Godolphin,** however, having risen in public office under the later Stuarts and 'neo-Stuarts' was made a Knight of the Garter in 1704 and an Earl in 1706. The arms as shown illustrate the practice of encircling the shield with the Garter. Also shown is an Earl's coronet and a barred helmet of the type reserved by the English Heralds for peers of the realm. The dolphin crest is intended as a pun on the name, but as previously mentioned does not illustrate its true derivation.

fig. 73   **Jonathan Trelawny,** 1650–1721, is the subject of the patriotic Cornish song, being one of the seven Bishops imprisoned by James II for refusing to read the Declaration of Indulgence. His arms, too, are shown encircled by the Garter, for although he was not himself a Knight of that Order he was, as

fig. 74   Bishop of Winchester, the Order's Chaplain. (Arms and crest engraved thus on pewter plates—R.I.C.) The shield shows the arms of the See of Winchester impaling those of the Trelawny family, the latter bearing the sinister hand device of a baronet. The whole is ensigned with his Bishop's mitre, this being the usual practice for high clerics, who did not display the military helmet and crest.

fig. 75   **John Anstis,** 1669–1744, M.P. for St Germans and later for St Mawes and for Launceston, was created Garter King of Arms in 1718. He was thus in charge of the English heraldic establishment, under the Earl Marshal, and was most energetic in furthering the claims of the College of Arms. His son, another John, also became Garter King of Arms.

In spite of the elder John's insistence on the College's authority, it seems the arms he himself used were adopted without a formal grant. These were 'argent, a cross raguly gules, between four Cornish choughs proper', the crest being 'a Cornish chough proper, resting the dexter foot on a besant'. Although these arms are very similar to those of the College of Arms they were used by him at least seven years before he became Garter, and he described them as being associated with the Anstis family.

The younger John obtained an official grant in 1740. In this the arms were similar but the new crest consisted of a plume of five ostrich feathers issuing from a King of Arms' coronet. Strangely, the elder John was kept in ignorance of this grant, which was not actually registered until some time later.

(See the article by David Bewes in the March 1987 Journal of the Cornwall Family History Society).

Garter has a multiple role as a member of the Royal Household in charge of ceremonial, as senior herald of the College of Arms, and specifically as King of Arms of the Order. He too has the right to display the Garter around his shield of arms if desired.

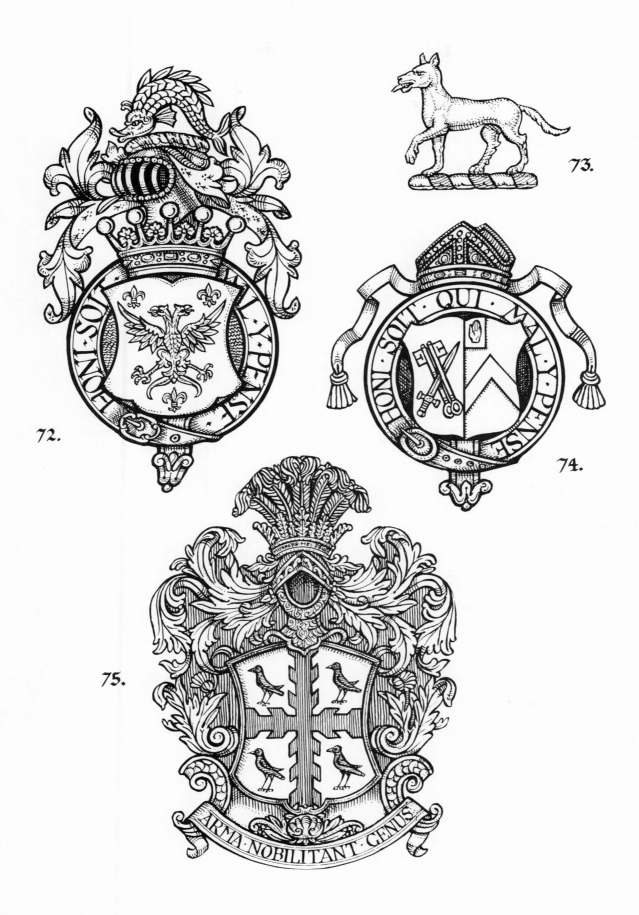

72.

73.

74.

75.

The French Wars

The 18th and 19th centuries produced many prominent military and naval figures, including a number of Cornishmen. Some were awarded 'augmentations' or additions to their arms in recognition of their services. Sometimes the designs leave much to be desired, including as they do realistic representations of war medals and more or less naturalistic battle scenes, far removed from the simplicity of ancient heraldry. Such arms are, nevertheless, full of historical interest.

fig. 76   **John Hockin, of Godrevy, Gwithian.** Although he was no military or naval commander, these arms include a gold lion on a red ground, and one could reasonably conclude that this was an official augmentation, derived from the royal arms. However, this was a simple grant of arms made in 1764 to John Hockin of Lydford in Devon to commemorate an exploit of his Cornish grandfather. The latter repelled single-handed an attempted landing by men of a French privateer on the coast near Hayle. The design of the arms clearly refers to the disarrayed French ('confusedly dispersed' fleurs-de-lys) and the lion-hearted John and his musket. The shield, of fanciful outline, is based on that illustrated in the original grant. The whole story is set out in the grant, and one wishes that this practice were more often followed. (See 'The Coat of Arms', 1960. Article by Colin Cole—presently Garter King of Arms.)

fig. 77   **John Harris Nicolas.** The heraldry of this Fowey family, of Huguenot origin, varied considerably at different periods. The original Breton arms included wolf's heads, while the arms illustrated were newly-granted in 1816 to John Harris Nicolas, commemorating his naval exploits. The naval crown, deriving from ancient Roman models, has been much used in the arms of prominent sailors and in the devices of naval establishments, etc. The wreath, trident and pennant are also clear references to a naval career.

fig. 78   **Lord Vivian of Truro.** This is a good example of the augmentation of arms anciently borne. Those of Vivian in the first and fourth quarters are basically as used by Prior Vivian of Bodmin in the 16th century. The 'embattled' chief and its wreath and campaign medals refer directly to Lord Vivian's service in the Napoleonic Wars, and in particular to his role in the decisive cavalry actions at Waterloo. The crest and supporters, representing troopers of various cavalry units, are certainly full of interest for military historians, but illustrate the difficulties for the heraldic artist required to represent members of particular regiments in correct uniform, particularly if the exact period is not specified.

76.

77.

PILOT

PATRIA CARA · CARIOR FIDES

VIVE REVICTURUS

78.

Cornish Seamen

Cornishmen figured among the many notable seamen of the 18th and 19th centuries who gained distinction in the French wars and in other activities worldwide.

fig. 79 **Admiral Edward Boscawen,** second son of the 1st Viscount Falmouth.

The arms illustrated show the simple ancient device without augmentation or additional quarterings.

Admiral William Bligh, born in Devon of Cornish stock, is known chiefly in connection with the 'Bounty' mutiny of 1787.

fig. 80 The name Bligh is said to derive from Cornish blyth—a wolf, but the arms feature a griffin.

Admiral Edward Pellew, first Viscount Exmouth, born at Dover of an old Breage family. He took part in many actions against the French, but is noted chiefly for his successful attack on Algiers and the release of Christian slaves there in 1816.

fig. 81 Though ancient Pellew arms are known, those shown are entirely different, being symbolic of his naval career. The 'chief' and the crest are more-or-less naturalistic representations of naval actions, and thus typical of the 'non- heraldic' type of augmentation of the period. At that time they would have been represented as unashamed realistic seascapes, but modern renderings tend to be more stylised.

79

80.

81.

DEO ADJUVANTE

ALGIERS

'Decadent' Heraldry

This term is sometimes applied to styles adopted after heraldry left the battlefield, which have been regarded as alien to the true spirit of heraldry. Enthusiasts for mediaeval heraldry have described as decadent the type of crest that could exist only as a two-dimensional representation and could never have been modelled in the round for use on a helmet. Similarly condemned has been the representation of a crest resting on a horizontal wreath bar, with the helmet omitted. The use of naturalistic instead of stylised forms is also often deplored. Shields were often shown in fanciful shapes, often surrounded by baroque or rococo decoration, foliage, etc., unlike any shield ever actually in use.

Another post-mediaeval development was the inclusion of multiple quarterings, representing families allied to the main line by marriage. This often resulted in a patchwork-quilt effect, in which the principal family was represented only by the first of dozens of quarterings. Such a shield can be extremely colourful and full of genealogical interest, but would be completely unsuitable on the battlefield.

All these features have been condemned by heraldic purists, but as works of art and craft much of such allegedly decadent work is of the highest order, and in any case is fully in accordance with the approved styles of its own period. Different ages have different artistic preferences and, as we have seen in connection with Victorian art, the pet hate of one generation may become the object of reverence and conservation of the next.

fig. 82   **Treffry of Fowey,** with 17 additional quarterings of Cornish families. From an 18th century Catalogue of Arms of the Nobility and Gentry of Cornwall. (C.R.O. Ref. DD.TF 1001.)

fig. 83   **Kendall, Bassett and Borlase,** from engraved bookplates in the collection
fig. 84   of the R.I.C.
fig. 85   The style of heraldic art work is left very much to the artist concerned, so long as the blason, i.e. the technical description, is adhered to. Some misunderstanding exists on this point, and some holders of official grants, particularly civic bodies, are under the mistaken impression that any subsequent representation should necessarily be a faithful reproduction of the painting on the original document.

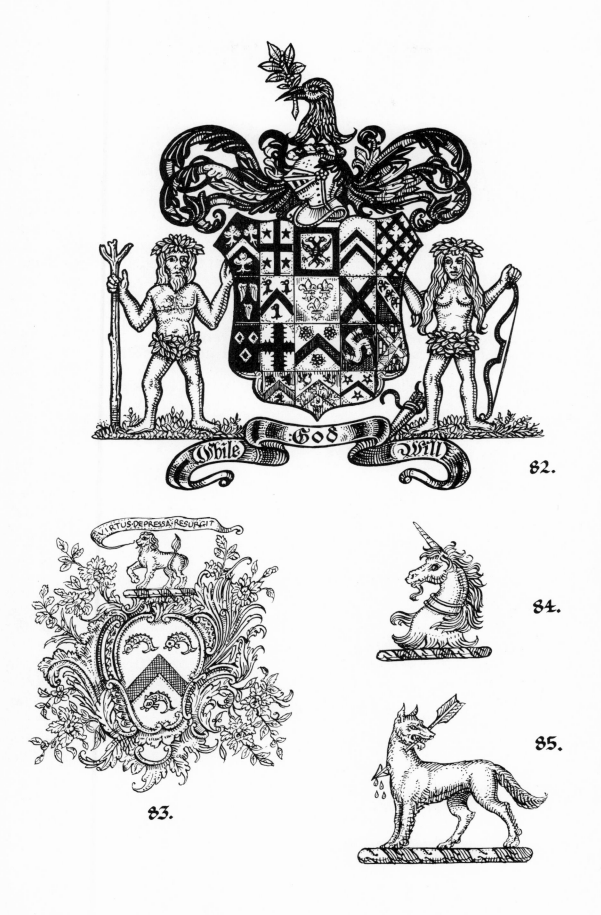

82.

VIRTUS·DEPRESSA·RESURGIT

83.

84.

85.

Trades and Crafts

Despite heraldry's original association with nobility, arms were at an early date granted to or assumed by individual burgesses engaged in trade and by trade guilds, and arms and similar devices have always been used in commercial contexts.

Trade Tools. Ecclesiastical architecture and furniture sometimes feature devices showing the occupation of the donor, and in some cases these are simple groups of craft tools rather than the arms of the relevant guild.

fig. 86   Carvers' implements on one of a number of medallions—Ruan Major. (Blight)

fig. 87   Smiths' implements on one of a number of shields, presumed to be on a former screen donated by Ralph Clies, master smith—St Ives. (Blight)

Merchants' Marks. Were similar in some respects to our modern trade-marks, and were used in mediaeval and Tudor times principally for marking merchandise. Though often barely distinguishable as such, the basis of many is a form of cross combined with the owner's initials. From their strictly practical use developed their employment as personal symbols, and we find them displayed in architectural settings, on tombs, etc., much as actual coats of arms were. Furthermore, such marks often appear on a form of shield.

fig. 88   Merchants' marks on brass shields, accompanied by matrixes of figures,
fig. 89   on a memorial stone—St Stephen by Launceston.

Trade Tokens. Mainly in the 17th and 18th centuries it became the practice for tradesmen to issue tokens, similar to coins, partly to remedy the shortage of official small currency and partly as a means of advertisement. Some tokens bore the arms of the relevant trade guilds, or a simplified version thereof, though the particular trader would not necessarily be a freeman of that guild. Other traders placed their own arms on their tokens, though in some cases these would appear to be self- assumed or those of another family of the same name.

fig. 90   Token of Mathew Rowett of Truro, 1668. A simplified version of the arms of the Mercers Company.

fig. 91   Token of Thomas Spry of Penryn, 1667. Arms of Spry impaling arms of Melhuish.

(See 'Cornish Tokens'—J. A. Williams)

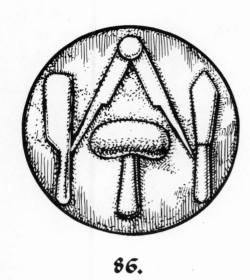

86.

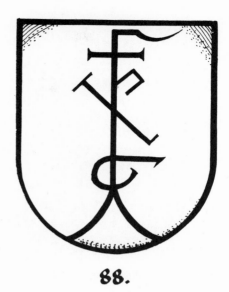

88.

87.

89.

90.

91.

Commemorative Ceramics. Individuals and bodies often commissioned specially decorated tableware, etc. for presentation or for use at functions.

fig. 92   **Liverpool Pottery Jug,** made for Richard Sampson of Penzance, trading 1820. This bears the arms of the Cordwainers Company of London, which were also used by the equivalent body at Exeter. The cordwainers took their name from Cordovan leather, and the goat's heads represent the goatskin which was one of their main materials. The supporters, tradesmen with footwear, do not appear in the official coat of arms. The tinctures indicated by the hatching and stippling in this design differ from the official version in that they show a blue chevron on gold, instead of vice versa. (R.I.C.)

fig. 93   **Liverpool Pottery Jug,** c. 1800. This bears a quasi-heraldic device consisting of a shield surrounded by roses and leaves. The various sections show a rowing boat, three fish, and fishermen with a seine net. A chevron over-all bears three roses and two cockleshells.

     This must have been made for one of the seine-fishing fraternities or partnerships, many of which bore the name 'Rose'. Clearly the roses in the design refer to this, though the origin is in the Cornish 'ros', signifying a net, and incidentally a circle. (R.I.C.)

fig. 94   **Swansea Pottery Plate,** c. 1800. This bears the device of a pilchard above the word 'Unity', the whole surrounded by the popular willow pattern. Part of a dinner service made for the Unity Pilchard Cellar at Newquay. (R.I.C.)

Silversmiths and Pewterers Marks

Silversmiths, Truro, late 16th to 17th cty.

fig. 95   An anchor.
fig. 96   TR monogram within besants.
fig. 97   A pig with a bell at the neck.

Pewterers

fig. 98   John Hoskyn of Truro—a lion rampant to the sinister, c. 1720.
fig. 99   Williams of Falmouth—a lion rampant to the dexter, c. 1720.

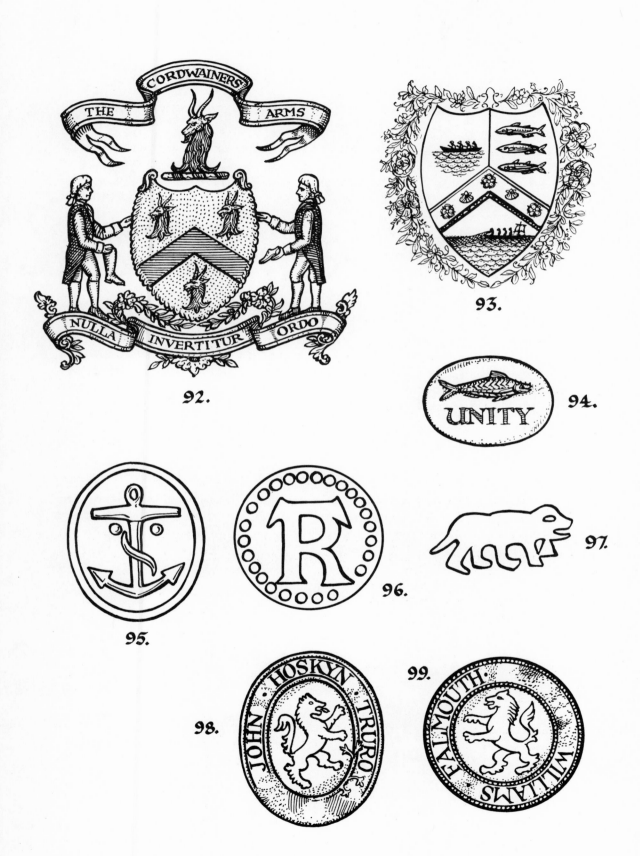

92.

93.

94.

95.

96.

97.

98.

99.

Mining

Pre-eminent among Cornish commercial enterprises, mining provides many examples of the use of distinctive emblems.

fig. 100   **The Stannaries.** From ancient times the Stannaries had privileges enshrined in custom and law. Their Common Seal, granted by Edward I in 1305 shows two miners at work with pick and shovel, accompanied by the Royal device of a lion's head. The letter N appears reversed in each case, an error on the part of the seal engraver. (R.I.C.)

Smelting House Devices. These were used for marking tin ingots, and there is a wide range of examples on display at the R.I.C. Most houses used
fig. 101   either the Pelican or the Paschal Lamb, both ancient Christian emblems, also
fig. 102   used widely in heraldry. The Pelican is often shown wounding itself to feed its young on its blood, as described in ancient bestiaries. This, like the Paschal Lamb, represents the sacrifice of Christ to redeem mankind.

fig. 103   A more individual design was that of the unicorn's head, used by the Portreath Smelting House. This was in fact the crest from the coat of arms of Francis Bassett, Lord de Dunstanville, and is also included in the recently-adopted device of Camborne Town Council.
(See also under 'Military Insignia' for the full Bassett coat of arms.)

fig. 104   **Mines.** Mines run on the 'cost-book' system would hold periodic Count-House dinners, often using cutlery and ceramics marked with the mine's name.
     Poldice Mine device on earthenware plate, c. 1925. (R.I.C.)

fig. 105   **Miners Association and Institute of Cornwall.** This body was formed in the late 19th century as an amalgamation of the Association and the Institute. Their device was a shield bearing the 15 besants of the Duchy, together with a group of mining tools. The illustration is based on part of an engraved advertisement for James and Company, Mine Engineers of Grampound, in Kelly's Directory of 1889.

     Though not forming part of the device as such, the miner 'supporter' is in the long heraldic tradition of single or paired figures accompanying a shield.

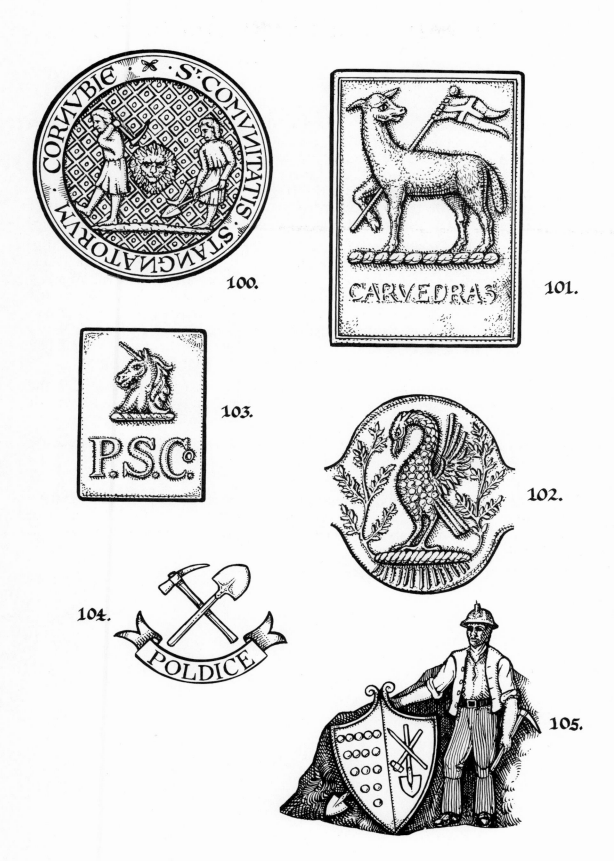

100.

101.

103.

102.

104.

POLDICE

105.

Railways and Other Industries

Most of the Railway Companies founded in the 19th century used devices on seals and on passenger rolling stock, etc., many being of an heraldic character. Sometimes new devices were adopted, but usually the Companies made use of the arms of towns served by their routes. This use of civic arms by commercial companies was completely irregular, as the appearance of a town's arms ought to imply that the enterprise was under the auspices of the local authority concerned, which of course is not so.

fig. 106   **Cornwall Railway Company.** The seal design includes the arms of the Duchy ensigned with the Heir Apparent's badge of the three feathers and coronet, commonly but incorrectly referred to as the 'Prince of Wales's feathers'. Below the shield appears the motto 'One and All', while draped around it is a fishing net, accompanied by tools associated with fishing and mining. This design is very reminiscent of the way in which coats of arms were sometimes shown draped with a mantle or robe of estate. (See 'The Story of Cornwall's Railways', A. Fairclough, Tor Mark Press, 1970.)

fig. 107   **West Cornwall Railway.** The shield device on this seal incorporates the ancient arms or semi-heraldic emblems of Truro, Penzance, Falmouth and St Ives.

fig. 108   **Helston Railway Company.** Apart from the encircling name of the Company the design of this seal is virtually the same as that used by the Borough of Helston.

fig. 109   **Borough Arms Foundry, Penzance.** The device of St John the Baptist's head on a charger is taken from the ancient seal device of the Borough of Penzance, and even the style of 'garter' or buckled strap around it follows that used on Borough stationery, etc.
(From an advertisement in Kelly's Directory, 1883.)

106.

107.

108.

109.

Inventors and Engineers

Cornwall has produced its prominent men in peace as in war, in particular in the fields of invention and engineering.

fig. 110 **Sir Humphrey Davy,** born at Ludgvan in 1778. One might have expected him to bear a version of the ancient Davy arms of Cornwall, but he was granted arms based on those of Davy of Norfolk, with which family there was presumably no connection. The distinguishing features in this case are the flame encircled by a chain, symbolising his invention of the miners' safety lamp, and the baronet's device of a sinister hand.

fig. 111 **West,** of St Erth. These arms are a reference to the smith's trade, ironfounding and engineering in general. William West, senior, 1751–1831, was originally a smith.
('Mead of St Gluvias and collateral families'. C.R.O. ref. AD 377/3.)

fig. 112 **Trevithick.** The arms of the St Eval family of this name. There has been speculation that the famous Richard Trevithick was connected with this family, but no actual proof. With such a distinctive Cornish name there is always the possibility of a link, but there are in fact several places bearing this name, any of which could have given rise to several non-related families.

fig. 113 **Richard Tangye,** born at Illogan in 1833, established with his brothers a flourishing engineering business in Birmingham. He was active in religious and local political life and as a philanthropist, and was knighted in 1894. The arms bear the sable border with besants seen in so many Cornish arms. The illustration shows a baronet's badge of a sinister hand, included in the arms of Richard's son, Harold Lincoln Tangye, when he was created a baronet in 1912. The full-faced open helmet is the type officially allowed with the arms of knights and baronets.
(Burke's Peerage, 1932, etc.)

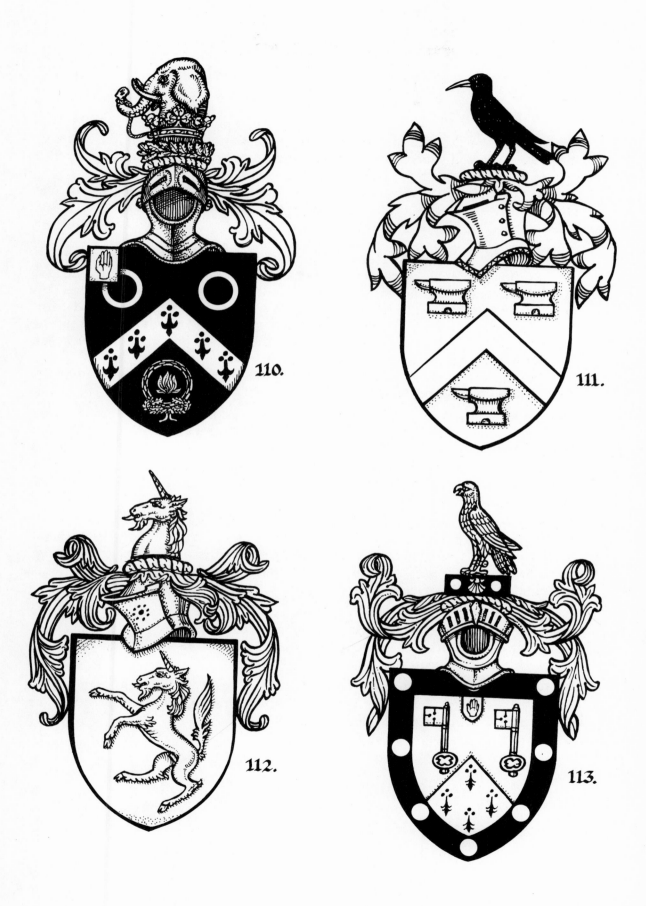

110.

111.

112.

113.

Civic Arms and Devices

When it became the custom for civic bodies to adopt arms and similar devices, these were often displayed on shields, sometimes with helmet and crest, etc., just as were the arms used by military leaders.

A number of municipalities received grants of arms from the Royal Heralds, but many contented themselves with adopting for their seal devices self-assumed arms, or emblems which can only loosely be described as heraldic.

Formerly the ancient chartered boroughs were the chief users of civic devices, but any legally incorporated body of sufficient standing could and can petition for a grant of arms. As before, in modern times the devices used by District and Parish Councils, etc. ranged from officially granted and fully heraldic arms, through semi-pictorial compositions resembling arms, to simple 'logos'. It is often these latter, with their stress on simplicity and easy recognition, that most truly reflect the spirit of ancient heraldry.

Modern changes in the pattern of local government have resulted in certain arms having become obsolete after only a brief use.

fig. 114   **Borough of Launceston.** The arms appear as illustrated in the original surviving grant dated 1573. Many civic arms bear castles, sometimes of a standard stylised form or sometimes, as in this case, a more or less representational rendering of the actual castle concerned. The lion in the crest is that from the arms of Richard, Earl of Cornwall, and the ostrich plumes are from the badge of the Heir Apparent.

fig. 115   **Camelford.** The camel fording a river is a fair example of the type of 'canting' or punning device favoured by mediaeval and Tudor heralds and designers. The river name Camel has quite other origins, being derived from the Cornish word cam—crooked. Although a shield is shown here, this is recorded as a seal device and not officially as a coat of arms.

fig. 116   **Grampound.** This is a more literal design, being a portrayal of the actual 'grand pont' or great bridge which gave the Borough its name. (In Cornish—pons mur). The shield of arms displayed on the bridge is that of Richard, Earl of Cornwall.

fig. 117   **St Ives.** This shows another punning device, again on a shield but not an official coat of arms. Likewise, the use of an ivy branch ignores the true origin of the name, which derives from St Ia.

114.

115.

116.

117.

fig. 118   **West Looe Trust.** A banner, designed in recent years, is based on the ancient Borough seal device of an armed man bearing a bow and arrow. Also included is the frequently used black border with besants, which in this case refers both to the Duchy of Cornwall and to St Christopher, to whom the ancient chapel at Looe was dedicated.

fig. 119   **Ladock Parish Council.** Only rarely have arms been granted to parish councils but many have adopted emblems for general use or, as here, for display on the Chairman's chain of office. A number of Cornish/Celtic saints are associated with holy wells and here we have Ladoca, the allegedly vain local saint, with a stylised chapel building and the heraldic symbol for a well or fountain.

fig. 120   **Kerrier District Council.** This is typical of many semi-heraldic devices of civic bodies. The representation of Carn Brea Castle has long been used as the emblem of Redruth, and the St Michael device is taken from the ancient seal of Helston. The base shows emblems of local industry and natural resources.

fig. 121   **Carrick District Council.** This is a stylised representation of a Carrick knot. Though the place-name Carrick and that of the knot are not connected, the former deriving from Cornish carreck—rocky, this fittingly represents an area with such a strong maritime tradition. The knot is variously shown vertical or horizontal in different contexts.

118.

119.

120.

121.

fig. 122 **Liskeard R.D.C.** A modern coat of arms, officially granted. The motif of two birds on a fleur-de-lys derives from the old Borough seal, while the 'chief' illustrates agriculture and commerce.

fig. 123 **Bude–Stratton U.D.C.** Modern arms, officially granted, illustrating the coastal location and Cornish connection. The chief bears two clarions or lance-rests from the arms of the Grenvilles, prominent in the area, and a cross pattee, from the arms of Sir John Berkeley of Stratton, the noted participant in the Battle of Stamford Hill, 1643.

fig. 124 **Newquay U.D.C.** Modern arms, officially granted, combining four herrings, representing local fishing activity, and a St Andrew's cross. The motto is a Cornish one, 'Ro an Mor' (Gift of the Sea).

fig. 125 **St Columb.** A non-heraldic device which is nevertheless striking and appropriate. A hand supports a silver ball, as used in the local hurling.

122.

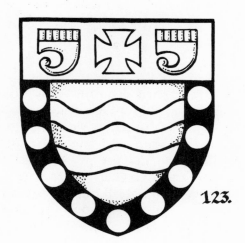

123.

124.

125.

Military Insignia

All heraldic devices are in a sense military, but here we deal only with those of regular and volunteer units associated with Cornwall since the 18th century. These units were very numerous and have been dealt with thoroughly in 'Military Insignia of Cornwall' and its Supplement, the work of Charles Thomas and the present writer.

Briefly, these devices conform generally to the standard patterns used by British army units. The bugle-horn was used by most rifle and light infantry units in Cornwall as elsewhere, this being the means of transmitting orders in such units. Emblems of specifically Cornish relevance are the Duchy arms of fifteen besants, often with the motto 'One and All', which appeared on the helmet plates, etc. of the Cornwall Rifle Volunteers and the Duke of Cornwall's Rangers Militia, and the castle and lion device from the later Stannary seal, featured on the buttons of the Duke of Cornwall's Light Infantry.

The Heir Apparent's badge of three feathers, coronet and 'Ich Dien' motto was also used on Volunteer tunic buttons, yeomanry helmet plates, etc. This device appears in connection with Welsh regiments and others bearing the title of, or otherwise connected with, the Prince of Wales. The Heir Apparent is usually Duke of Cornwall from birth, and only later created Prince of Wales at the Monarch's discretion, so this three-feathers device is to that extent more appropriate to Cornwall than to Wales.

Some of the small volunteer units used devices of local reference, as did Home Guard units of World War II.

fig. 126   **Penryn Volunteers Medallion or Token.** (1794). This bears on the obverse the ancient Saracen's head seal device of the Borough of Penryn with a trophy of weapons, and on the reverse the complete achievement of arms of Lord de Dunstanville. (R.I.C., and M.I.C. No. 235.)

fig. 127   **Scillonian Fencibles Button.** (1798–1800) The dolphin crest of the Godolphins, Lords Proprietors of Scilly from 1549 to 1831. (Island Museum, Scilly, and M.I.C. No. 241.)

fig. 128   **32nd (Cornwall) Regiment Shoulder Belt Plate.** (c. 1810?–1832) A standard type with the regimental number and title, surmounted by a crown. This regiment became the first battalion of the Duke of Cornwall's Light Infantry in 1881. (D.C.L.I. Mus. and M.I.C. No. 15.)

fig. 129   **Pendennis Artillery Button.** (1808–1828) The Volunteer units of that period were given the title Royal Cornwall Local Militia. As one would expect, a number of artillery units were stationed at Pendennis. (M.I.C. No. 168.)

fig. 130   **Royal Devon and Cornwall Miners Button.** (Pre 1852) The Duchy arms accompanied by the Heir Apparent's badge and the unit title. The lion supporters to the shield are very unusual, and seem to have no official recognition, but they do also appear with the Duchy arms on the Stannary Court building at Lostwithiel. (J.S.A.H.R. 1936 and M.I.C. No. 149.)

126.

127.

128.

129.

130.

fig. 131   **Cornwall Artillery Volunteers Pouch Belt Plate.** (1861–1908) The Duchy arms within an elaborately scrolled border surmounted by the Heir Apparent's badge, and with the title on a scroll beneath. (M.I.C. No. 175.)

fig. 132   **Cornwall Rifle Volunteers Waist Belt Plate.** (1870–1882) The Duchy arms and Heir Apparent's badge, laurel wreath, title and motto 'One and All'. This motto has no official recognition as part of the Duchy arms but is universally used and appears in Cornish military contexts from the early 19th century. (M.I.C. No. 259.)

fig. 133   **Duke of Cornwall's Light Infantry Officer's Helmet Plate.** (1881–1902) The Light Infantry bugle-horn is combined with the castle from the later Stannary seal and two crossed red feathers. These latter represent the 46th (South Devon) Regiment which was incorporated as the 2nd Bn D.C.L.I. in 1881. They are a reference to the regiment's part in a battle at Paoli in the American War of Independence. The standard elements for officers helmet plates of the period were the Garter with motto, the unit title on a scroll, a laurel wreath and 8-pointed star. The 'Victorian' type of crown was replaced by the 'King's' type in 1902. (M.I.C. No. 82.)

fig. 134   **Falmouth Volunteer Submarine Miners Pouch Badge.** (1888–1892) This engineers unit used as a badge the crest of the Board of Ordnance, a hand issuing from a mural crown and grasping a thunderbolt. This makes a most appropriate device for a unit whose function was to protect Falmouth Harbour by means of electrically detonated mines. (M.I.C. No. 189 and Meade.)

fig. 135   **Duke of Cornwall's Light Infantry Collar Badge.** (1881–   ) This officer's version is in gilt metal with black enamel. The coronet and arms of the Duchy with 'One and All' motto. (M.I.C. No. 89.)

fig. 136   **Duke of Cornwall's Light Infantry Cap Badge, etc.** (1899–1959) A stringed bugle surmounted by a Royal Duke's coronet with 'Cornwall' on a scroll. This device was used in numerous contexts but was probably best known as a cap badge, in white metal with a red cloth backing. The latter again refers to the 46th Regiment. This badge was discontinued in 1959 when the regiment was amalgamated into the new Somerset and Cornwall Light Infantry, later itself to become the first battalion of the Light Infantry. (M.I.C. No. 108.)

131.

132.

133.

134.

135.

136.

High Sheriffs of Cornwall

A High Sheriff is one of the few individuals who at least up to very recent times actually required a coat of arms, in this case for display on the official banner, as well as on his seal of office. Normally this officer would be chosen from the level of society in which arms were used, whether or not these were officially granted.

fig. 137 **Richard Lobb.** (1652) He was one of those who held office under the Commonwealth. Although the College of Arms was essentially a Royal foundation, it was continued at this period, and these arms were allegedly granted then. The official College records do not mention these arms, so presumably they were not confirmed at the Restoration. A token of his, used at Falmouth in 1655, bears three boar's heads, and on the reverse three trefoils.

('20,000 Lobbs Round the World', D. Lobb, 1985.)

fig. 138 **Francis Gregor.** Three of this name held the office in 1669, 1716 and 1788. They were of a Truro merchant family which rose to gentry status, acquiring Trewarthenick at Cornelly. The arms are canting or punning. Gregor as a surname presumably derives from the baptismal name Gregory, but 'gruk-yar' signifies a partridge (literally heather-hen) and three such birds appear in the arms.

When the male line of the Gregors died out, the heiress married a member of the Booker family who changed his name to Gregor and adopted new arms with elements from those of both families. A number of other Cornish families now bear names which were assumed by the incoming husband of an heiress to a substantial estate. In some cases a hyphenated name represented both families, but often the husband's family name was abandoned altogether.

fig. 139 **Elizabeth A. Johnstone.** (1983/4) The arms are shown on a lozenge or diamond, as is the usual practice for ladies. They are a differenced version of those of the Chief of the Name in Scotland.

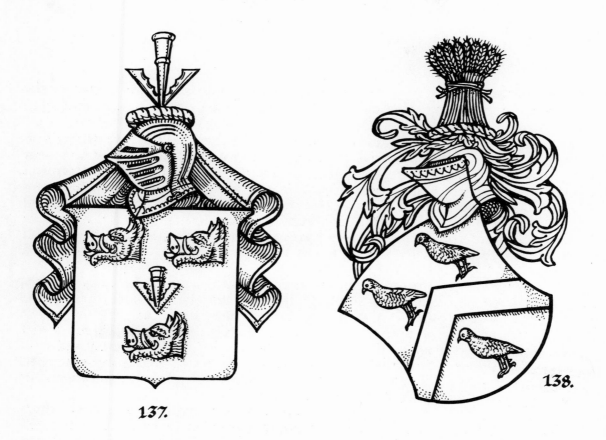

137.

138.

139.

Canting Arms

This term is applied to those arms which make some word-play or pun on the family name, having some reference to its real or imagined origin or simply to its sound.

In some cases the allusion is obvious, but sometimes the pun depends on the inclusion of objects or creatures which formerly had names now no longer in use. Again, the pun may be in an unfamiliar language. Thus in Cornwall one or more roses frequently appear in the arms of families whose names include 'ros' or 'rose'. This is a good pun in English or Cornish as 'rosen' in Cornish does signify a rose, though in most if not all these names this element derives from 'ros', a place-name element signifying a promontory or high heathland. Occasionally it appears to be a corruption of 'res', signifying a ford.

fig. 142

Other Cornish canting arms depend on a knowledge of Latin or French, as in those of Tremayne. Similarly the Trestain family bore three stone columns, whereas the name originates in 'tre' plus 'sten', tin.

fig. 140
fig. 141

The arms of a number of these 'Tre' families include three similar objects, and this may be because 'tre', a homestead, has been confused with 'try', signifying the number three. However, the reason may simply be that, as in many other examples, three objects make a very satisfactory arrangement on the form of shield most commonly used.

Among the most interesting examples of canting arms are those which depend on a knowledge of the Cornish language. In cases where a Cornish word is similar to its former or present English equivalent, it is not always possible to say which prompted the choice of design, but in some cases the Cornish language reference is clear. Again the design does not always illustrate the true origin of the name, but simply includes objects whose names in Cornish suggest the sound of the name. The origin of place names is in any case a complicated matter and subject to a good deal of surmise.

figs 144–155

This use of Cornish in what was then such a prestigious context as a coat of arms seems to show that the language was held in some regard, and certainly not, at least at the time the arms were adopted, despised as mere peasant speech. It would be interesting to discover the actual date of adoption of each of these Cornish canting arms in relation to the extent of Cornish-speaking at the time. Some were certainly in use in the 16th century, being described in Baring Gould's 'Armory of the Western Counties' dealing with mss. of that period. Some are known from the Heralds' Visitations of the 16th and 17th centuries. Some may well have been in use much earlier.

This practice still continues, and a number of such canting coats of arms and other family emblems have been granted or adopted in modern times.

fig. 152

At least one example of canting arms relies on Cornish dialect as opposed to true Cornish. The arms of Harvey of Linkinhorne include three harrows, 'harve' meaning to harrow.

Many British families in the past used Latin or French mottoes with their arms, but some of Irish, Welsh, Scots or Manx ancestry have used their own Celtic tongues for this purpose. Similarly some families used Cornish language mottoes, and in modern times this practice continues both with family devices and with the emblems of civic bodies and associations of all kinds.

140

fig. 140   **Tremayne.** Clearly an allusion to three hands, French 'trois mains', this has no connection with the true origin of the name, which is presumably from tre-men or tre-meyn, signifying homestead of the stone, of stone, or of stones.

fig. 141   **Trestain.** Three stone columns, but probably from 'tre sten', homestead near tin workings.

fig. 142   **Penrose.** Three roses, but probably from 'pen ros', end or top of promontory, heathland.

fig. 143   **Trefusis.** Three fusils, but possibly from 'fossow', entrenchments.

fig. 144   **Cleather.** Three swords. 'Cledher'—sword.

fig. 145   **Keigwyn.** 'Ky gwyn'—white dog, but possibly from 'ke gwyn'—white hedge.

fig. 146   **Trembleth.** 'Blyth'—wolf.

fig. 147   **Gregor.** 'Gruk yar'—partridge, literally heather- hen, but the name is presumably a form of Gregory.

fig. 148   **Molenick.** Greenfinch or goldfinch.

fig. 149   **Trenethyn.** 'Edhen'—a bird.

fig. 150   **Treweek.** 'Whek'—sweet.

fig. 151   **Trevisa.** 'Ys'—wheat.

fig. 152   **Harvey.** 'Harve'—dialect to harrow, but probably from Breton 'haer-vy' meaning battle-worthy.

fig. 153   **Whetter.** 'Whether'=Blower, i.e. hornblower, or worker in a blowing or smelting house.

fig. 154   **Endean/Indian.** Two of the many forms derived from 'an den', the man.

fig. 155   **Penberthy.** A gorse bush. 'Perthy'—bushes.

141.   142.   143.

144.   145.   146.   147.

148.   149.   150.   151.

152.   153.   154.   155.

Cornish/Celtic Organisations

The Cornish Gorseth. The principal device used by the three allied Gorseths of Wales, Cornwall and Brittany is the 'awen', comprising three radiating shafts of light. A number of meanings are attributed to this, but it is essentially a symbol of divine inspiration. It also represents the direction of the rising sun's rays at the eastern cardinal point and at the longest and shortest days of the year.

fig. 156 The central device shown is adapted from the Gorseth banner, displaying the awen in gold on a bardic blue ground, and surrounded by the distinctively Cornish border of besants.

fig. 157 The Gorseth regalia is largely made of hand-beaten copper, as in the Grand Bard's crown, Marshals' staves, and horn- mounts shown here. The ceremonial sword represents Arthur's Excalibur, but is never fully drawn, emphasising the Gorseth's peaceful aims.

fig. 158 The motto is a Cornish rendering of that also used by the Welsh Gorseth, 'The truth against the World'.

fig. 159 **Cowethas An Yeth Kernewek.** The Cornish Language Association device is a man's head in profile with a scroll bearing the word 'Kernewek' issuing from the mouth, stressing the association's special encouragement of the use of the spoken language. It also refers to the Cornish language periodical 'An Gannas', The Messenger.

fig. 160 **Pan Celtic.** This body is concerned with inter-Celtic musical and other cultural activities. The circular device includes the stylised figure 6, and the letters P and C, representing the six Celtic countries and the association's title. The form is reminiscent of the ancient symbol of the tryskel.

fig. 161 **Cuntelles Keltek** (Celtic Congress). The six components of the circular device of Celtic knotwork represent the six Celtic nations. The banner is white with the device in white on a purple roundel.

fig. 162 **Ros Keltek** (Celtic Circle/Wheel). This dance group's emblem also makes use of Celtic knotwork decoration with a surrounding circle, suggesting the complicated but orderly movements of traditional dancing.

156
157
158

159.

160.

161.

162.

Society Banners

The heraldic banner is strictly a square or rectangular flag carried on a staff and bearing throughout its area the elements of the shield device of some prominent individual, originally of a military commander. However, the word banner has also been widely used for other forms, e.g. hung from a cross-staff or on two staves. The cross-staff type has always been a popular means of displaying the devices of, for example, trades guilds and religious bodies, particularly in processions.

This ecclesiastical use has continued into modern times, and similarly such bodies as the Old Cornwall Societies, Mothers' Union, Women's Institutes and Young Farmers' Clubs all have their branch banners. Though often of a semi-heraldic character, these tend to include lettering and pictorial elements somewhat alien to true heraldic design. Nevertheless they are often of great interest, including references to local history, topographical features, etc.

fig. 163   **St Austell Old Cornwall Society.** The small crosses on the shield symbolise the ten churches in the area, and these surround a stylised china clay mound bearing the shield device long used by the Borough of St Austell. This appears originally to have been the coat of arms of the Austell family, and bears two 'ragged staves', possibly a pun on the Cornish word astell, signifying a board or shingle. Above the shield is the Cornish chough and the motto in Cornish, 'King Arthur is not dead'. Below the shield is the Cornish version of the society's title, and below this, again in Cornish, 'Cornwall for Ever'.

fig. 164   **Penryn and Falmouth Old Cornwall Society.** The main feature is a map of the area, based on a Tudor original, and in front of this a representation of the 'Marlborough' Packet. Above is the motto in Cornish 'One and All', and below is the society's title. The whole is surrounded by traditional Celtic interlacing.

fig. 165   **Kea Women's Institute.** This comparatively simple but effective design features the Kea plum.

fig. 166   **Penpol and Point Women's Institute.** The four quarters represent the following:
The lamb-and-flag emblem of the Penpol Smelting Works, formerly situated on the shore of Penpol Creek.
The Schooner 'Rhoda Mary' built last century by Ferris Brothers at Penpol Boatyard.
Penpol or Point Quay, one of the oldest buildings in Point.
The arms of the Duchy.
At the centre is the white cross of St Piran bordered with black.

mygh teyn arthur nyns yu marow

COWETHAS KERNOW GOTH
SENT AUSTLE

Kernow Bys Vyken

163.

ONEN HAG OLL

H.M. PACKET MARLBOROUGH

PENRYN & FALMOUTH
OLD CORNWALL
SOCIETY

164.

KEA W.I.

165.

PENPOL & POINT

166.

Other Cornish Associations

fig. 167   **Cornish Guild of Heralds.** The uprooted oak-tree symbolises family history and the dispersal of many Cornish families overseas. It bears a shield with the device of St Piran, and beneath it is the motto in Cornish 'Land and Family'.

fig. 168   **Royal Cornwall Yacht Club.** When founded this had as its Patron the Prince of Wales, Duke of Cornwall, later Edward VII. Thus, the cap badge bears the Heir-Apparent's triple plume of feathers encircled by a coronet. The burgee is blue, bearing the Heir-Apparent's plume and coronet, in this case all in white.

fig. 169   **Cornish–Welsh Society.** The Cornish chough and Welsh dragon face each other on a grassy mound.

fig. 170   **Newlyn Male Choir.** A quarterly shield bears 1. A Mount's Bay lugger with the coastline in the background; 2. The device of St Piran; 3. A stylised lyre; 4. The Newlyn Pier and Light.

fig. 171   **Cornish–Breton Twinning Association.** A Cornish chough and an ermine support a shield bearing the device of St Piran and the ermine spots of Brittany. In this case the scrolls bear the names of the twinned communities of Truro and Morlaix.

fig. 172   **Cornwall Family History Society.** The oak-tree is used by many such societies to symbolise growth, and the branches of a family. A shield of the Duchy arms is suspended from the tree and in the flanks are a top-sail schooner and a mine engine-house, typifying the Cornish scene.

167.

168.

169.

170.

171.

172.

Seals and Livery Buttons

The use of arms, crests, monograms and other devices was particularly popular in the 18th and 19th centuries. The opportunity for heraldic display was very limited for most families and was largely confined to use on signet rings, fob seals, notepaper, and to a lesser extent on plated tableware and servants' livery buttons.

fig. 173   **Seal Impression—Neils B. Falck.** He was Danish Consul at Falmouth in the 18th century and his official seal bears his personal arms of a perched and hooded falcon, supported by the figure of Mercury, the god of commerce.

fig. 174   **Livery Button—Falck.** This family of Danish origin settled in Falmouth and became prominent there in the 18th century. The punning falcon appears again in the crest, here issuing from a coronet.

fig. 175
fig. 176   **Seal Impression and Livery Button—Gay.** William Gay was the last director of the Falmouth packet service in the early 19th century. This family was allied to that of Falck, and it is likely that the falcon in the crest derives from this source. The escallop shell is derived from those appearing in the arms of this and other families of the name of Gay.

fig. 177   **Livery Button—St Aubyn.** A baron's coronet above the crest of Lord St Levan of St Michael's Mount—a chough rising from a rocky mound.

fig. 178   **Livery Button—Hodson of Fowey.** This crest illustrates one of the problems of latter-day heralds, that is the designing of new arms and crests sufficiently different from the thousands already in use. The lion has so often been used, that it became necessary to show it holding various objects, and/or resting a foot on them, as a means of distinction.

173.

175.

174.

176.

177.

178.

Family Devices

With the great upsurge of interest in family history, there have been formed various associations of those researching a particular name. In some cases they cover all families of the name even though there may be no reason to suppose any actual relationship.

Some of these 'One-Name' Societies have adopted devices which include motifs taken from the coats of arms of bearers of the name. Others have chosen emblems to represent the name's presumed or actual origin.

fig. 179   **The Uren Society.** The chough or raven and the lion's face are from the arms of Urren. The inscription signifies 'The Uren Family' in Cornish.

fig. 180   **Tangye.** A personal device illustrating the presumed origin of the name, i.e. Cornish/Breton tan-gy, signifying fire-dog.

fig. 181   **The Harry Family Group.** The sea-dog is from the ancient arms of Harry of Cornwall.

fig. 182   **Harvey.** This device is based on the derivation haer- vy, signifying battle-worthy in Breton. A Celtic warrior is surrounded by the inscription in Cornish signifying 'To Arm Without Aggression'.

179.

180.

181.

182.

Schools

Occasionally schools and colleges obtain official grants of arms, or rather their governing bodies do so in their capacity as legal corporations. Many more simply adopt 'badges', often indistinguishable from coats of arms, and in some cases actually being the arms of the school's founder. Others incorporate elements of the arms or other devices of a local authority. This practice of adopting quasi-heraldic devices is sometimes the cause of complaint by sticklers for heraldic authority, but is so frequent and long-established that very few schools would consider paying the substantial fees required for a grant.

fig. 183   **Truro School.** The upper devices of an open book and a dove, symbolising the Holy Spirit, allude to the fact that the school was founded with the intention of providing a religious (Wesleyan) basis for the education offered. In some versions the dove and book appear separately above the shield.

fig. 184   **Richard Lander School.** This design alludes to Richard Lander's birth-place, later known as the Dolphin Inn. The dolphin in this case is in its more natural non-heraldic form, and also serves as a symbol of intelligence. The wavy barrulets refer to the River Niger, and the border of besants emphasises the Cornish connection.

fig. 185   **Duchy Grammar School.** The open book, here on a sky- blue 'chief', is a frequently used symbol of learning. The inclusion of the fifteen besants from the Duchy arms was in this case specifically authorised, but these have appeared in many school and other devices without any official permission, nor indeed any official objection.

fig. 186   **Perranarworthal Primary School.** This design was adopted on the occasion of the School's centenary and refers in a straightforward way to St Piran, to Perranwell village, and to learning.

fig. 187   **St Stephen in Brannel School.** This recently adopted device includes the arms of former Lords of the Manors of Brannel and Bodinnek, the Earls of Cornwall and the Carminow family, together with the open book. The palm branches refer to the martyrdom of St Stephen.

183.

184.

185.

186.

187.

The Cornish Chough

With its distinctive colouring of black with scarlet bill and legs the chough has always been popular in heraldry, and understandably appears in many coats of arms of Cornish families. It was frequently used elsewhere, however, notably in the arms later attributed to St Thomas à Becket. In fact, choughs were occasionally described as beckets in blasons of arms, or there may have been intended a pun on 'beak'.

At least some twenty Cornish families have borne three choughs in their arms, either alone or accompanied by some other simple charge, for example:

fig. 188 **Trevener.** Argent, a chevron sable, between three Cornish daws volant proper.

fig. 189 **Spore.** Argent, three Cornish daw's heads erased proper.

fig. 190 **Tregeare.** Argent, a fesse sable, between three Cornish choughs proper.

More recent uses include the following:

fig. 191 **Newquay Battalion, Home Guard.** In World War II this unit used a yellow shoulder flash bearing a chough, and this also appeared on their flag, which survives at Trerice.

fig. 192 **Duchy of Cornwall.** In modern times two choughs have been officially recorded as supporters to the ancient arms of the Duchy, each bearing an ostrich plume in allusion to the fact that the title is normally held by the Heir Apparent.

fig. 193 **Cornwall County Council.** The crest is a chough resting its dexter claw on a coronet, the whole upon a 'torse' or wreath of the colours of the arms. The crest may appear alone above the shield or upon a helmet with its mantling.

The coronet is presumably a reference to the Duchy, and the type shown is indeed rather misleadingly described by heralds as a 'ducal' coronet. However, other distinct types are allocated to dukes in general, royal dukes, and the Duke of Cornwall as Heir Apparent.

188.

189.

190.

191.

192.

193.

The Duchy Coat of Arms

Every so often the argument arises as to the origin and meaning of these arms, providing a recurring subject for correspondence in the Cornish press.

Firstly, we may dispose of the 'fifteen balls' as an inn sign. The objects are in fact flat discs, not spherical, and are heraldically described as besants. This name derives from the coins of ancient Byzantium, and they are found in the arms of a number of modern banks and finance houses. However, in many coats of arms there seems to be no special reference to money, the besants being used merely as decorative motifs, just as are roundels of other tinctures.

William Camden, a herald under Elizabeth I, describes Cadoc, Earl of Cornwall, as bearing a black shield with besants. We do not know what evidence he had, or if there was some surviving tradition of such use. Possibly the idea was simply suggested by the existing Duchy arms. If any of the early Cornish rulers did indeed bear such a shield it would probably have been of a pre-heraldic form, bearing bronze or gilded bosses as decoration or added protection.

fig. 194

In early examples the number of besants shown was not fixed, and some that survive have numbers ranging from twenty-two on the border of a sculptured shield of Richard, Earl of Cornwall (died 1272) in Westminster Abbey, fourteen and eleven respectively on two of this same Richard's seals, seventeen on Edward V's state sword (1483), and ten on the tomb of Elizabeth I, also in Westminster Abbey.

fig. 195

fig. 196

This last example is the first we know of that shows the besants in the now familiar triangular form ('in pile' as the heralds have it).

On the Great Hall at Lostwithiel the arms have the rare addition of two lions as supporters. The carving itself probably dates from the 17th century and is one of the earliest examples having the fifteen besants in pile. This has since become the accepted pattern, and is now officially recorded as such. The arms appear thus on John Speed's map of Cornwall of 1611.

fig. 197

fig. 198

Cornwall County Council, having over a long period used the plain Duchy arms, now bears officially granted arms, which are a differenced version, including a border with alternate argent and azure wavy barrulets.

A. L. Mata, writing on the subject in 1929, disposed of many groundless stories concerning the origin of the besantee shield, while making a number of controversial comments of his own! However, we may accept his arguments that it was adopted at the time of the creation of the Duchy for Edward the Black Prince in 1337, and that the besants have no known significance beyond being derived from the arms of Richard, Earl of Cornwall.

Versions of these arms have been used by numerous Cornish organisations, schools, military units, etc., sometimes with the colours changed. Also granted to or assumed by a number of Cornish families was a black border with besants, but this occurs elsewhere with apparently no Cornish significance. Technically the black shield with fifteen besants is that of the Duke of Cornwall as such, and not for general use. It appears in his full achievement of arms, along with other elements denoting his position as Heir Apparent and Prince of Wales.

The besants on a sable ground may be interpreted as a symbol of mineral wealth obtained from the dark depths of the earth. This would certainly be appropriate for Cornwall, but there is no evidence that this, or indeed any other interpretation, provides the original reason for adopting the besants.

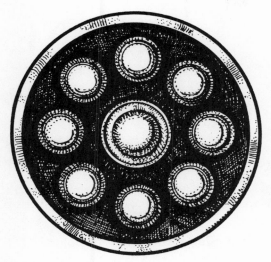

194.

196.

195.

197.

198.

Recent Cornish Arms

The arms shown are of comparatively recent adoption, being granted by or recorded with various heraldic bodies.

fig. 199   **Barfett.** A differenced version of the ancient Barfett/Trebarfoot arms. Bear's feet form a punning device, though there is no suggestion that this is the origin of the name.

fig. 200   **Billing.** A Celtic wheel-cross added as a difference to the ancient Billing arms.

fig. 201   **Bray.** Horse-brays were instruments used to control unruly horses, and have been borne by a number of families of this name. In this case the bearer, being of the London Scriveners Company, has included their device of an ink-horn and penner. The name Bray has various suggested origins, but in Cornwall probably comes from 'bre', signifying a hill.

fig. 202   **Geach.** Many ancient arms included three scallop shells, and to provide a sufficient difference from these this design shows them on an arched chief and on a fesse, with the further distinguishing device of an axe.

fig. 203   **Jenkin.** The single charge in the ancient arms of Jenkin of Cornwall is a lion rampant and regardant, i.e. looking to the rear. In this instance substantial differencing is achieved by placing a golden fret over the lion and adding a chief bearing a Bardic oak-leaf crown between two scallop shells, the latter representing the maritime element in the ancestry.

fig. 204   **Roseveare.** Punning arms incorporating roses. The name probably derives from 'ros vur', signifying a great promontory, but as 'rosen' is Cornish for a rose, the pun holds good in both Cornish and English.

fig. 205   **Elvins.** The main device of the lion and the lozenges or diamonds is virtually the arms of the maternal family of Turnham, but the addition of the four 'St Elvin's crosses' makes this a new and distinctive coat.

fig. 206   **Trythall.** Clear references to a Navy career are the basis of this design. The familiar border bears as a variation alternate besants (gold) and plates (silver), the total being of necessity an even number.

fig. 207   **Skews.** Arms were borne by a number of Cornish families of this name and elements from these are incorporated in this new design.

199.

200.

201.

202.

203.

204.

205.

206.

207.

Suggested Devices

No doubt new arms, badges and other emblems will continue to be adopted by individuals and bodies associated with Cornwall, and the following are suggested as being suitable and appropriate. Some of those shown have already been used, usually in conjunction with others.

The first group represents elements in family names, which are themselves often derived from place-names.

fig. 208 The chevron, being a particularly effective motif when used on the normal triangular shield, has been widely used in heraldry. Often it seems to have no particular significance, but it has been regarded, in its resemblance to roof timbers, as a symbol of a building. Thus it can be used to stand for such Cornish name-elements as 'tre'—homestead, 'chy' or 'ty'—a house, 'bod' or 'bos'—a dwelling, etc. The Cornish word 'keber' does in fact mean both a chevron and a roof timber, just as in French the word chevron stands for a rafter or an heraldic chevron. The chevron is used so often that this 'couped' version provides a useful and distinctive variation.

fig. 209 In heraldry, a roundel bearing alternate white and blue wavy bars represents a fountain, well or pool, and thus may stand for such Cornish name-elements as fenten, pol, etc.

fig. 210 A division of the shield 'per chevron' may represent *pen*—a headland, hilltop or promontory, or *ros*—a promontory, the base representing one of these features and the upper area representing sky or water as appropriate.

fig. 211 The division of the shield 'per fesse embowed' may represent *bre*—a hill, *hal*—a moor, etc.

fig. 212 A division 'per chevron inverted' may signify *nans* or *nant*—a valley.

fig. 213 The element *ker* or *car*, signifying a fortified camp, may be represented by a division 'per fesse embattled'.

fig. 214 *lan*—an enclosure, here represented by an 'orle', a border at a distance from the edge of the shield.

fig. 215 *ke*—a hedge, is here represented by an embattled border.

fig. 216 *res*—a ford, may be represented by two or more 'bendlets wavy'.

The second group represents materials or objects associated with mining, or with Celtic tradition.

fig. 217 The alchemical symbol for tin.
fig. 218 The alchemical symbol for copper.
fig. 219 A kybel or metal mine bucket.
fig. 220 A Celtic wheel-cross.
fig. 221 The tryskel.
fig. 222 Tin ingots.
fig. 223 A Cornish shovel-head.

The fact that some of these devices are rare or previously unknown in heraldry makes their use the more desirable.

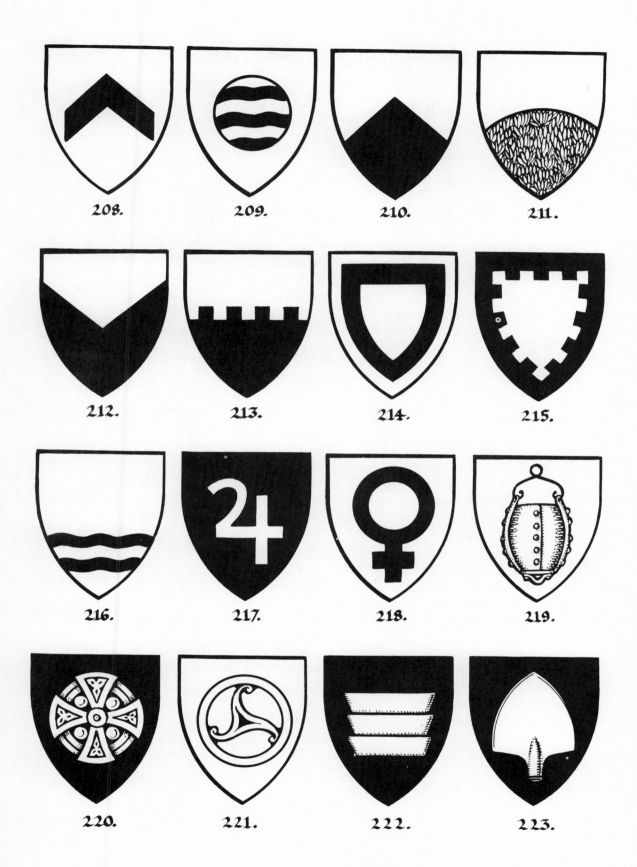

208.

209.

210.

211.

212.

213.

214.

215.

216.

217.

218.

219.

220.

221.

222.

223.

Plant Symbols

We have already touched on the use of the oak, yew and mistletoe in the context of early Celtic symbolism.

Cornish Plant Emblem

In recent times there has been some discussion on the choice of a plant emblem to represent Cornwall, and recently the Gorseth Council recommended the use of Cornish Heath (Erica Vagans) for this purpose, as being indigenous and possibly unique to Cornwall. This has some disadvantages in that it is difficult to render in a stylised way, and moreover is not easily distinguishable from other varieties by the majority of Cornish people.

Some use has been made of the gorse as a Cornish emblem. This is easily recognisable and lends itself to formal representation. It has also been claimed (by many of the Cornish themselves, be it said) that it represents a certain prickliness in the Cornish temperament! The gorse forms part of the device of the recently formed Cornwall Heritage Trust.

Corn Dollies

Here we may glance only briefly at this subject, researched in some depth by Jan Gendall. Their use is certainly not confined to Cornwall, but there are local variations in types and in customs.

Briefly, a corn dolly was made from the last straw reaped at a Harvest, the cutting of which involved the ceremony of 'Crying the Neck'. After this a feast was held, called 'Gooldize' or 'Gooldice', signifying the feast of the ricks.

Many more or less intricate patterns occurred, traditionally associated with different areas. The dolly was sometimes saved until the following Harvest, and in Cornwall it was given at Christmas to the best milch cow or best bullock on the farm.

Another class of dolly was smaller, being given as a love token, one type being in the form of a ring through which a man and his girl would kiss.

Many symbols and rituals have been loosely classified as having fertility significance, but the corn dolly clearly does come in this category.

fig. 224	Stylised Gorse Emblem.
fig. 225	St Neot Dolly. 4ft 6in. or higher.
fig. 226	Polperro Dolly. Approx. 24in. high.
fig. 227	Polzeath Dolly. 20in. to 24in. high.
fig. 228	Nancledra Dolly. 16in. to 20in. high.
fig. 229	Kissing Ring. 2in. to 3in. diameter.
fig. 230	Love Knot. Approx. 3in. long, 1in. diameter.
fig. 231	Truro Dolly. Approx. 20in. long.

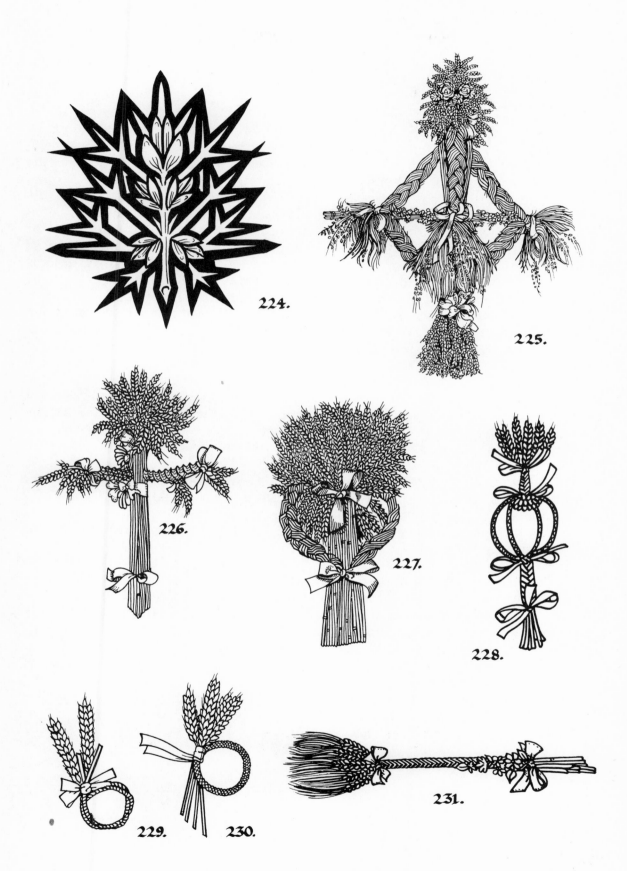

224.

225.

226.

227.

228.

229.

230.

231.

Tartan

Among the distinguishing characteristics of the Celtic peoles noted by classical writers was the use of garments variously described as of striped, chequered and variegated patterns. Likewise, Celtic works of art such as the Book of Kells show figures in checked or tartan-like dress.

The more recent historical use of tartan is usually associated with the Highlands of Scotland. Particular designs or 'setts' became popular in different districts and later came to be associated with the different clans or extended families. Some of these setts are of great antiquity, but most of those known today are of more or less recent origin, and in fact new designs continue to be produced. From being the mark of the highlander tartan came to be regarded as a symbol of the whole of Scotland. Its use has spread even further in later times, and new tartans have been designed for the provinces of Canada, the Royal Air Force, and the Commonwealth Games, for example.

The characteristic of true tartan is that the sequence and proportion of colours is the same in both weft and warp, though there are exceptions.

With the introduction of relatively inexpensive textile weaving in the 19th century tartan became very popular, purely as decoration, in the dress of Victorian ladies and also worldwide, especially in the Far East, for both male and female clothing. Of interest in this connection are the hand-woven shawls of tartan or quasi-tartan design worn by West Cornwall fisherwomen in the 19th century.

The Cornish National Tartan was the first to be introduced here in modern times, in fact some twenty years since, by E. E. Morton Nance. The symbolism of its colours is as follows:
Black and gold—the colours of the Duchy arms and traditionally of those of the ancient Celtic rulers of Cornwall.
Black and white—from the device of St Piran.
Black and red—the colours of the chough.
Blue—for the sea surrounding Cornwall.

More recently, three other Cornish tartans have been introduced, i.e. a 'hunting' version, predominantly dark blue and green, a 'day' tartan with lighter blue and gold, and a 'St Piran' tartan, largely in black and white. The common feature in all four is the inclusion of white lines crossing black areas to suggest the St Piran cross.

Though of recent introduction the use of Cornish tartans is spreading rapidly and adding a colourful dimension to the Cornish scene and to Cornish/Celtic events, here and worldwide.

The Use of Heraldry and Symbolism Today

Life would surely be poorer without the decorative and useful symbols and emblems that appear all around us. There is a general acceptance of the idea that national, public, commercial and voluntary bodies should identify themselves by such means. At the same time, despite the widespread interest in heraldry proper, it cannot be maintained that this enjoys the same prestige that it did in former times.

Nowadays, although there is a general reluctance to classify people socially, there are still identifiable those in public life who would certainly have used armorial bearings as a matter of course in an earlier age. Many of these are now indifferent or even hostile to the idea of personal heraldry, which is no longer considered an essential adjunct to a prominent position in the life of the nation. For example, it is no longer a cause for comment that a peer may be non-armigerous.

The actual use to which a personal or family coat of arms can be put today is very limited, beyond perhaps on a bookplate or as a modest wall display. Even those bearing arms by descent or grant may be loth to make much use of them.

Consequently, the obtaining of a grant or the assumption of arms is often inspired by an interest in the subject of heraldry and genealogy as such, rather than as being the normally accepted social custom. As interest in these subjects grows, more individuals and families feel the need of some such symbol, be it a coat of arms or the emblem of a family association, and in modern times social or occupational status is becoming largely irrelevant in this connection.

We may be sure that whatever changes may occur in social life or ideological thought, the study of the history and art of decorative symbols will continue to be of absorbing interest to many.

CAREW. The arms of the family of Richard Carew of Antony, whose Survey of Cornwall of 1602 gives such a valuable insight into Cornish life of the period. Blasoned as 'or, three lioncells passant in pale sable, armed and langued gules', they are reminiscent of the royal arms of England, but are sufficiently distinctive in that the lions are black on gold with their heads facing dexter instead of towards the onlooker. The crest, 'a mainmast, the round-top set off with pallisadoes or, a lion issuing thereout sable', seems a rather cumbrous decoration to surmount a helmet. It may indeed never have seen actual use in this role, but many known tournament crests were certainly of very fanciful design and large proportions.